The Economic Impact of the Welfare State and Social Wage

The British Experience

RAFAT FAZELI

Avebury
Aldershot • Brookfield USA • Hong Kong • Singapore • Sydney

© R. Fazeli 1996

All rights reserved. No part of this publication may be reproduced, stored in a retrieval system, or transmitted in any form or by any means, electronic, mechanical, photocopying, recording or otherwise without the prior permission of the publisher.

Published by
Avebury
Ashgate Publishing Limited
Gower House
Croft Road
Aldershot
Hants GU11 3HR
England

Ashgate Publishing Company
Old Post Road
Brookfield
Vermont 05036
USA

British Library Cataloguing in Publication Data

Fazeli, Rafat
    The economic impact of the welfare state and social wage
    1. Welfare state - Economic aspects 2. Public welfare - Great Britain - Economic aspects
    I. Title
    330.1'26

ISBN 1 85972 157 5

Library of Congress Catalog Card Number: 96-83711

Printed and bound by Athenaeum Press, Ltd., Gateshead, Tyne & Wear.

Contents

Figures and tables vii
Acknowledgements xii

Introduction 1

1 The origin and the development of the welfare state 7

2 The literature on economic boundaries of the welfare state: The legitimacy of the welfare state and economic growth 31

3 Empirical studies on the distributional impact of the state budget 46

4 The welfare state and the reproduction of the working population: The study of the social wage in the United Kingdom 70

5 The results and the concluding analysis 113

Appendix I The estimation of the net social wage for the working population with and without adjustment for the self-employed and the top managers 140

Appendix II The estimation of the net social wage for the working population and the self employed 146

Appendix III The trend of the net social wage for the working population and the self employed: Excluding the share of the top managers 149

Appendix IV The estimation of the net social wage for the

		working population with indirect business taxes	152
Appendix V		The estimation of the net social wage for the working population and the self-employed (Indirect business taxes included)	157
Appendix VI		The trend of the net social wage for the working population and the self employed: Excluding the share of the top managers (Indirect business taxes included)	160

Bibliography   163

Figures and tables

Table 3.1	Net benefit/ tax position of households, 1971	51
Table 3.2	The net impact of state benefits and taxation on the income of households, 1976	53
Table 3.3	Gini coefficients of vertical inequality	55
Table 3.4	Flows between the personal and state sectors, 1975	60
Table 3.5	Sources of workers' consumption: The wage and the citizen wage, 1948-1977, in constant (1967) dollars	63
Table 3.6	The percentage share of workers' consumption and capital in total output	66
Table 4.1	Public expenditures trends	82
Figure 4.1	The share of transfer payments in total expenditures and in GNP	83
Figure 4.2	The share of social security in total expenditures	84
Figure 4.3	The share of social security in labor income	84
Figure 4.4	The share of public assistance and welfare in total expenditures and in GNP	85
Figure 4.5	The share of public assistance and welfare in labor income	86

Figure 4.6	The share of housing in total expenditures and in GNP	89
Figure 4.7	The share of housing in labor income	89
Table 4.2	Periodization of public expenditures programs	91
Table 4.3	Post-war cycles	92
Figure 4.8	The share of health in total expenditures and in GNP	93
Figure 4.9	The share of education in total expenditures and in GNP	95
Figure 4.10	The share of public utilities in total expenditures and in GNP	97
Figure 4.11	The share of transportation and communication in total expenditures and in GNP	98
Figure 4.12	The share of taxes on wages and salaries in total taxes	101
Figure 4.13	The share of social security and payroll taxes in total taxes	101
Figure 4.14	The share of taxes on wages and salaries in labor income	103
Figure 4.15	The share of social security benefits in labor income	103
Figure 4.16	The share of taxes on wages and salaries in total labor taxes	104
Figure 4.17	The share of social security and payroll taxes in total taxes	104
Figure 4.18	The share of other taxes in total taxes	105
Figure 4.19	The share of taxes on immovable property by households in total taxes	105

Figure 4.20	The share of taxes on property estate, gift, wealth inheritance in total taxes	107
Figure 4.21	The share of taxes on corporate profits and capital gains in total taxes	107
Figure 4.22	The share of taxes on goods and services in total taxes	111
Figure 5.1	Transfer payments, social expenditures, and civil public consumption	114
Figure 5.2	Transfer payments, social expenditures, and civil public consumption as percentage of GNP	114
Figure 5.3	Total labor taxes over labor income and total labor social benefits over labor income	115
Figure 5.4	Net social wage ratio adjusted for self employed and unemployment rate	115
Table 5.1	Public expenditures trends	118
Table 5.2	Periodization of public expenditures programs	122
Table 5.3	Post war cycles (economy and social expenditures)	123
Figure 5.5	Government budget deficit and net social wage	128
Figure 5.6	Government budget deficit minus net social wage	128
Table 1.a	The measurement of the net social wage (Adjusted for the top managers)	140
Table 1.b	The measurement of the net social wage (Adjusted for the top managers)	142
Table 2.a	Benefits and taxes paid by labor (Adjusted for the self employed)	143
Table 2.b	Benefits and taxes paid by labor (Adjusted for the self employed)	144

Table 2.c	Benefits and taxes paid by labor (Adjusted for the self-employed and top managers)	145
Figure II.1	Total labor taxes over labor income and total social benefits over labor income	146
Figure II.2	Net social wage ratio adjusted for self employed and unemployment rate	147
Figure II.3	Government budget deficit and net social wage	147
Figure II.4	Governement budget deficit minus net social wage	148
Figure III.1	Total labor taxes over labor income and total labor social benefits over labor income	149
Figure III.2	Net social wage ratio (adjusted for top managers and self employed and unemployment rate)	150
Figure III.3	Government budget deficit and net social wage	150
Figure III.4	Government budget deficit minus net social wage	151
Figure IV.1	The share of indirect business taxes in labor income	152
Figure IV.2	The share of social security and payroll taxes in total labor taxes	153
FigureIV.3	The share of taxes on wages and salaries in total labor taxes (Indirect business taxes excluded)	153
Figure IV.4	The share of total labor taxes (with indirect business taxes) in labor income and total labor social benefits in labor income	154
Figure IV.5	The share of indirect business taxes in total taxes	154
Figure IV.6	Total labor taxes (with indirect business taxes) over labor income and total labor social benefits over labor income	155

Figure IV.7	Net social wage ratio (with and without public assistance and unemployment rate)	155
Figure IV.8	Government budget deficit and net social wage (with and without public assistance)	155
Figure V.1	Total labor taxes over labor income and social benefits over labor income (Self-employed and public assistance included)	157
Figure V.2	Net social wage ratio adjusted for self employed and unemployment rate	158
Figure V.3	Government budget deficit and net social wage (with and without public assistance)	158
Figure V.4	Government budget deficit minus net social wage (with and without public assistance)	159
Figure VI.1	Total labor taxes over labor income and total labor social benefits over labor income	160
Figure VI.2	Net social wage ratio (with and without public assistance and self-employed) and unemployment rate (adjusted for top managers)	161
Figure VI.3	Government budget deficit and net social wage (with and without public assistance)	161
Figure VI.4	Government budget deficit minus net social wage (with and without public assistance and self employed) adjusted for top managers	162

Acknowledgements

I would like to thank Anwar Shaikh whose astute suggestions and careful feedback have been indispensable for this work. I owe a debt of gratitude to Willi Semmler and Cyrus Bina for their valuable comments on various issues related to this book. I should also like to thank David Bragg, Director of the Computer Center, for his support to provide computer assistance in preparing the final manuscript. I am thankful to Katherine Hafeli, my research assistant at the University of Redlands, who assisted me in formating the final manuscript. Lastly, my thanks to Reza Fazeli for his intellectual support and comments throughout various revisions.

Introduction

State intervention in capitalist economies and its attempts to regulate the relations between capital and labor is hardly a new phenomenon. But these interventionary activities of the state evolved in the twentieth century and especially after World War II, against a background of sustained economic growth up to the mid-1970's. And while the term "Welfare State" might be misleading, it is not misleading to assume the liberal states in advanced capitalist countries have experienced some transformations to be explained.

The expansion of the social expenditures of the state faced little challenge in the period when capital enjoyed a high or normal rate of accumulation and economy a high or normal rate of growth. Whatever the source of welfare expenditures, its expansion required a growing economy. A simple transfer of surplus from capital to labor was never the objective nor a possibility for the so-called "Welfare State" within the framework of the capitalist relations of production. The expansion of these redistributionary expenditures might be financed, whether by an economic surplus (itself the product of a growing economy) or the wages of a large number of employed workers (a transfer from the employed to the unemployed or the old or the poor) and in either case was possible only with a high or normal performance of the economy. The plausibility of the social policy then required a host of other activities to retain the high level of employment and rate of growth. A sustained commitment to the provision of social services and social security required a successful economic policy to stabilize the economy. In this way, social policy was not the only function for the state in liberal democracies. The other component was Keynesian economic policy which was supposed to provide the state managers with the tools for a conscious intervention in the economy. The Keynesian "demand management", it was said, would enable the governments to achieve growth and full employment.

Keynesian economic theory also provided the social policy with an economic justification since in this model they would sustain each other. There was a widespread belief that the expansion of welfare expenditures would not be in any conflict with economic policy and would not endanger the success of its objectives. Conversely, it even could help the achievement of growth and full employment through its stimulating affect on the aggregate demand and even some measures of welfare expenditures acted as automotive or built-in stabilizers.

The low performance of the economy in the 1970's, the rising costs of social welfare programs, and the concomitant higher tax burden, stimulated strong reaction against both Keynesian economic policy and social policy especially in Britain and the United States. "By the end of the 1970's the OECD countries between them had the equivalent of the whole population of Yugoslavia (22 million) out of work with unemployment concentrated among the young and the disadvantaged" (A.H.Halsey in OECD 1981, p.14). This generalized recession struck almost all the advanced capitalist countries and this time was accompanied by a high rate of inflation. The high rate of inflation and the fiscal crisis of the state meant that the Keynesian-style expansionary deficit spending could no longer be considered as a sound economic policy. The increasing rate of unemployment accompanied by a downward pressure on real wages meant a higher cost of social security and welfare expenditures if the past standards of benefits were to be retained. But it was not only the expansion of the welfare state which came under attack. Every crisis always generates a massive attack on the share of labor. For the recovery of profitability, capital among other things pushes for a decline in real wages and benefits received by workers and the poor. This period experienced a substantial decline in the average rate of profit. In the United States, for example, profit of the non-financial corporations almost continuously declined from a peak of 17 percent in 1965 to 7 percent in 1980 and for the United Kingdom from more than 10 percent to below 6 percent in 1980 (Shaikh 1983, Mandel 1978: 22, 23, Glyn-Sutcliff 1971). The effect of this decline became more significant in this period because it undermined the amount of the total profit. The excess capacity build-up in this period was probably another sign. In the United States the ratio of manufacturing capacity utilization was 89 percent in 1965 and 68.7 percent in 1975 (Shaikh 1983).

Now the general consensus of the post-war period of boom attempting to moderate the ideological differences between capital and labor has been shaken. The last decade has evidenced the emergence and growth of what is called "neo-conservatism." "There is widespread loss of confidence in the capacity of states to deliver either full employment or welfare services." (A.H.Halsey in OECD 1981: 8). Keynesianism as an economic theory, as well as the political program of the social democratic and liberal parties, comes under attack. It is no longer the assured economic orthodoxy which it was and the orthodox economists are no longer all Keynesians.

In recent years, the Western liberal democracies have appeared to become more and more ungovernable because their governments are facing an "overload" of demands for rising social services that they cannot cope with. Radical critics have attributed the increased burden of the interventionist policy either to the accumulation function of the state in response to worsening economic crisis, or to increased costs of welfare programs aiming to maintain legitimacy and harmony for the state and the capitalist structure of society, or the successful struggle of the working population for expanded and improved social welfare services leading to the redistribution of resources from capital to labor. Conservative and Liberal critics, on the other hand, blame the "excessive expectations" and "inflating claims" of the electorate which, in their view, have led to unrestricted welfare state development to an extent that exceeds the fiscal capacity of the state.

In short, the contemporary debate has focused on the growth and crisis of public programs that have been associated with the rise and expansion of the welfare state. The other aspect of this debate is concerned with the interrelationship between the declining rate of economic growth of the last two decades, the higher level of inflation and unemployment and the fiscal crisis of the state induced by public expenditures. This debate regarding the limits of social policy and its crisis should be linked to the development of the welfare state and the social wage and its relationship with other aspects of the societal developments.

Marxian authors have shown more interest in a general class analysis of capitalist state activities and their role (or function) in the reproduction of the different aspects of the capitalist order. At this level of generality, the distinctive features of social policy in different phases of societal (or capitalist) development are overlooked. Such a general analysis can provide a general guideline for a more detailed study but can tell us little about the patterns of development of particular programs in a specific country and their qualitative differences with the previous forms of welfare policies (such as the poor relief programs) in the earlier history of Welfare Capitalism.

The neoconservative theoretical contributions, on the other hand, are profoundly ahistorical and asocial in their approach. In their critique of welfare state institutions and their economic boundaries they do not make any reference to the origin of the welfare state programs and those economic, social, and political developments which were influential in their particular patterns of development. The fatalist view that the only way out of the current crisis is the dismantling of the welfare state institutions and a total submission to the spontaneous market order, represents a disregard of the historical inadequacies of market institutions which led to the development of social programs in the first place. Their ahistorical approach has led them to present the market order in its ideal form, abstracted from its historical origin and development. The market order itself has not evolved spontaneously without the forceful intervention of the state and its development has led to the disintegration of the traditional forms of organizations which provided the earlier forms of welfare and relief. The development patterns of the welfare state have also been shaped by social and political developments. This means that while, in a capitalist society, the progression of welfare programs beyond certain limits may exceed the capacity of the state which is constrained by the private control of resources, the regression of social programs below certain boundaries can also cause problems for accumulation, social harmony, and political stability of the society.

It is therefore apparent that an analysis of the welfare state and its crisis requires the study of its development trends shaped by changes in economic constraints, political institutions, and social structures. The first Chapter of this book will concentrate on the development of the welfare state and social policy in Britain. This Chapter will trace the pre-history of the welfare state in Britain. The analysis of the early history of the welfare state will assist us to identify the distinctive features of modern social policies. The welfare state has often been characterized by its departure and differentiation from the repressive measures adopted in the poor relief policies of past centuries. A comparative analysis of these periods will allow us to address the question of whether the development of the modern welfare state presents a qualitative change in social policy and whether this change has led to any transformation of the basic structure of the British capitalist society and the relationship between the state and the socioeconomic system.

The emergence of the modern welfare state and its two Post-War II developments will be the subject of study in the last sections of this chapter. The first section of this Chapter will focus on the economic, political, and ideological developments which led to the transition from the Poor Law to the modern welfare state in Britain. In the last section the institutionalization of the "Keynesian welfare state" and its developments after World War II will be analyzed.

In Chapter two the boundaries of the welfare state and its relationship with the current crisis of the British economy will be discussed. We will pay particular attention to the contributions of these British authors and others whose views bear a relevance to the case of Britain. These views on the economic and social limits of the welfare state and the possible linkage between social programs' developments and the recent economic crisis will be presented in the context of three major paradigms: the Liberal, the Neoconservative, and the Radical. This will allow us to treat those theoretical contributions not merely as "value free" or "objective" models, the validity of which may depend on their internal consistency and persuasiveness, but a part of a broad theoretical approach and tradition representing certain world view and ideological trend, and yet not overlooking the significant distinctions and differences of individual theories belonging to each general approach.

In Chapter three, we will turn to the empirical contributions on the redistributive activities of the state. Two groups of studies will be critically reviewed. The first group includes the studies on "vertical" redistribution or redistribution among households in different income ranges. The second group includes those studies concerned with the development of the social wage or the redistributive impact of the state on the working population.

Chapter four will include our own empirical contribution. The empirical research of this stduy is concerned with the Post-War II development of the social wage and its economic and social boundaries. We have chosen the post-war period firstly, because the required data for prior history are lacking, and second because this period coincides with the emergence and the development of welfare state institutions in Britain.

The present study is concerned with the distributive role of the welfare state in the United Kingdom for the period of 1953-86, the period for which data have been available. The objective of this study is to examine the net benefit/burden position of the working population with respect to expenditures and taxes in this period. The empirical methodology of research will be laid out in this Chapter, and the results and the conclusions derived from these results will be presented in the last Chapter.

There are three major issues which this research will address. First, this book will provide a framework to analyze the growing significance of the "social wage" or the collectivization of consumption by the working population and the share of social consumption in their total consumption. This will help to provide a better understanding of the resource allocation in the private and the state sectors of the economy and to determine if the activities of the state have grown to become the substitute or just the complementary to private production of goods and services.

Second, the analysis of the social expenditures and the "net social wage" trends will allow linking the post-war development of the welfare state and social wage in Britain to other aspects of societal developments. The findings of this study will be used to determine to what extent the welfare programs' developments have been shaped by changing economic constraints and social and political conditions. These findings will also be analyzed to explore the possible interaction between the trends of social expenditures and the economic slow-down (or crisis) of the last two decades.

Third, the evidence presented in this book provides an empirical foundation to analyze and evaluate the validity of the major models on the crisis of the welfare state in the context of Britain. The evidence will be used to determine whether the growth of social transfer payments and social expenditures have led to the government "overload," as conservatives have suggested or to the "fiscal crisis of the state," as some radicals have predicted. The findings will also provide a basis to test the hypothesis that the continuous increase of the social wage or "citizen wage" has adversely affected the after-tax rate of profit and has consequently resulted in a slow-down in accumulation and economic growth.

1 The origin and the development of the welfare state

In this chapter we trace the origin of the welfare state in Britain. The institutionalization of the modern welfare state occurred after the Second World War and it was to some degree conditioned by the concrete developments during the war. This was nevertheless the product of several centuries of struggle over social policy conditioned by the general trends of capitalist development and industrialization. The link between the contemporary welfare state and other aspects of capitalist development in Britain can not be fully comprehended without an explanation of such historical developments. This historical review should also assist us to shed more light on some current debates on the (class) nature of the welfare state and to test the claim of those who argue that the policies of the welfare state go beyond the limits of capital accumulation and the capitalist structure of the distribution of power, resources and income. A comparison of the policies associated with the forms of social policy adopted in the earlier stages of capitalist development should help us to have a better grasp of such attributes of the welfare state.

I. The contrast between the Poor Law and the welfare state

What has been identified as the "welfare state" is basically a product of more recent developments during the last one hundred years. The start of the modern welfare state can be dated back to the last two decades of the nineteenth century during which the first national insurance programs of institutional importance were initiated in Germany, Britain, and some other Western European countries. The welfare state has, nevertheless, an important early history, the study of which would substantially promote our understanding of the nature of its contemporary role in industrially advanced capitalist societies. As Gaston Rimlinger (1971:59) has demonstrated, there is a need to distinguish between two phases of this "pre-history." The first phase is the "Poor Law" period from the sixteenth to the nineteenth century. The second phase starts with the "Liberal Break" of nineteenth century up to the Second World War and is a period during which the basis for the modern welfare state is built up.

Modern social policy is often characterized by its departure and differentiation from the principles dominating the poor relief measures of this early history. While the Poor Law provided a "relief of the poor within a framework of repression," contemporary welfare programs are usually perceived as a form of citizen's rights (or social rights) of the recipients (Rimlinger 1971 and Marshall 1964). The Poor Laws contained an element of reciprocal social responsibilities, but they were much more reliant on punishment than on relief. Both the Elizabethan Act of 1601 and the New Poor Law Act of 1834 were based on a national concern and reflected a national policy on the welfare and the relief of the poor but their point of reference was mainly the relationship between individuals and local communities and their execution was left to local authorities (see Flora and Alber 1982). The modern welfare policy, on the other hand, is carried out or at least directed by national institutions and incorporates a much higher degree of uniformity of the benefits.

The welfare state is thus defined more in terms of its differences from the Poor Law and not the similarities. Nowhere is this distinction postulated as conspicuously as in Marshall (1964: 80). He argues that in contrast with the welfare state, based on the principle of social rights, "the Poor Law treated the claims of the poor not as an integral part of the rights of the citizens, but as an alternative to them-as claims which could be met only if the claimants ceased to be in any true sense of the world". A similar notion has been put forward by Wilensky (1975: 6-7). He has held that, "the essence of the welfare state is government-protected minimum standards of income, nutrition, health, housing and education, assured to every citizen as a political right, not charity."

The difference between the welfare state in contemporary societies and its predecessors is exaggerated. When we introduce the notion of economic boundaries, we learn that in fact both the welfare state and the Poor Law system are constrained by certain limits. Even in a parliamentary-democratic capitalist society in which "citizenship rights" are fully developed, the material resources of state power and their allocation primarily depend upon the revenues generated in the accumulation process. This means that the introduction of social welfare programs and the extent of their development is considerably limited by accumulation requirements. During the Poor Law period, the relationship between the welfare policies of the state and accumulation appeared to be more direct and more conspicuously manifested. This relationship is not as apparent in more recent advanced capitalist societies. The achievement of civil and political rights has provided the working population with a means to pursue their demand for social services with a higher degree of legitimacy. The relatively crude ideology of the Poor Law period, legitimizing the emphasis of welfare policy on accumulation requirements, has been replaced by a more sophisticated value system taking into account not only the accumulation aspect but also the rights associated with citizenship and the formal equality of citizens with respect to social services. This implies that the relative autonomy of social policy from accumulation has considerably increased. It is no longer possible for the state to design a social policy serving merely the needs of the accumulation process. The pursuit of such a policy may undermine the legitimacy of the state.

There is therefore a conflict between the objectives of welfare state social policies, promoting the political stability and the legitimacy of the state, and the distributive rules and economic mechanisms of capitalism. But the modern welfare state is a product of capitalism. The objective of the welfare state is to provide a security net for individuals to cope with the unpredictability of the market system, but not to challenge its legitimacy. If the earning capacities of capitalism are entering a phase of stagnation, the limits of the development of social welfare become apparent. It is true that the logic of legitimation carried beyond a certain point may begin to come into conflict with accumulation. But the government may opt for accumulation and reduce those activities which are usually associated with the legitimation function.

As Mishra (1984: 88) has stated, "accumulation is one of the major sources of legitimation of the capitalist system." An economic depression with rising unemployment rate (and high rate of inflation such as the situation of the 1970's) can as well undermine the legitimacy of the state and the capitalist system. Such a condition may facilitate the revival of an ideology to an extent similar to the one of the Poor Law period legitimizing the higher degree of concentration of the state policy on accumulation and a cut-back in the welfare expenditures. The relative success of the New Right campaign against increasing welfare activities of the state and the rise of Thatcher and Reagan administrations in Britain and America exemplifies this possibility.

There are therefore both major differences and substantial similarities between the modern welfare state and the Poor Law system. The rise of the welfare state may be perceived as both the departure from and the continuation of the premises of state intervention during the Poor Law period. To the extent that society then and now remains a capitalist society, accumulation maintains its central importance in both cases. In both stages of capitalist development the ability of the state to carry out its programs depends on the fortunes of private capital. The two aspects of state activities, promoting stability and fulfilling the accumulation requirements, have continued to interact with each other, although the content of these two functions has considerably changed. But this change has been possible because the requirements of accumulation have changed. Rising productivity and increasing per capita output imply that the welfare state can afford to pay more attention to the provision of social and welfare services.

The actual transformation of social policy at certain historical moments (more or less by the turn of the century) has to be explained by such factors as the formation of the national state, its transformation into a parliamentary democracy, changes in the dominant ideology and ideas of welfare and poverty, the struggle of the working population, and the attempt of the state to integrate the working class without any fundamental challenge to the institution and distribution of private property and the means of production.

From the very beginning the role of social policy has gone beyond providing social harmony and political stability. The provision of relief and welfare was closely linked with the accumulation of capital. This is not only because the social welfare activities of the state have a significant effect on accumulation process, but also because from the early stages of capitalist development welfare institutions have been a pre-condition of the commodification of labor power.

As Marshall has acknowledged, a basic important civil right is the right or freedom to work at the location of the worker's choice. The recognition of this right was required to guarantee the free mobility of labor from one region to another or from one occupation to another. In feudal British society, the direct producers were bound to the land and did not have the right to accept other occupations. It was in the process of the enclosure movement that the direct producers were forcefully separated from their means of subsistence and consequently constituted the population of free laborers who had no property but their labor power to sell in exchange for wages. But even after the transformation of the mode of production from feudalism to capitalism, restrictions on free mobility of labor continued for a considerably long period of time. The further development of capitalism required the removal of these restrictions. The recognition of this right provided not only the conditions for free mobility of workers, but also the right of the employers to hire every worker without restriction.

Even though modern industry necessitates the variation of labor and the universal mobility of laborers because of contradiction between the technical necessities of this modern industry and the social character inherent in its capitalist form it prevents security in the situation of the laborer (Marx 1977, ch. 25:457). The commodification of wage-labor, on the other hand, required the involvement of the institutions which provided the non-commodity form of support for labor.

II. The rise of capitalism and the loss of subsistence

With the growth of commerce and woollen manufactures, an increasing number of the English landowning aristocracy proceeded to commercialize their holdings in the fourteenth and fifteenth centuries. This process led to the displacement of a large number of the peasantry who lost their rights to the land and became agricultural laborers. At the early stages of this development, the hiring terms of the dispossessed peasants were still considerably influenced by traditional feudal relations, and they were also able to keep their rights to the forests and commons. With the intensification of the commercialization of agriculture and consequently the transformation of land from tillage to pastures for sheep in response to the increasing demand for wool and from subsistence crops to cereal grains demanded by the population of the growing cities, the terms of employment became more starkly market-oriented (Piven and Cloward 1985: 47-8).

The mobility of the population was not a voluntary action by the peasants in search of opportunities and a better life in urban areas. They were forced into the labor market because the traditional nexus of work and subsistence had been broken and under the new circumstances subsistence was made conditional not on the readiness to work but on the chance of employment by those who owned and controlled the means of producing the valued goods. What this meant was that whereas under feudalism the peasant families starved or died when crops failed, now they could suffer the same fate if they were unemployed, even when the harvest was good. For those who were fortunate enough to find employment, the standard of living might have been better than that of the serfs. But their life chances were now more unpredictable and subject not only to the state of the harvest but also to the fluctuations of the market economy.

Sir Frederick Eden in his report on The State of the Poor (1797) wrote "to the growth of civilization and the development of commerce may be ascribed the introduction of a new class of men, henceforward described by the legislature as the poor" (see Marshall 1981: 27). This new class of poor were "the dispossessed, the masterless and the incompetent" who "were literally set in motion by irresistible forces as they sought first work that was not to be had and then alms which society was neither equipped nor disposed to give" (Jordan 1959: 55,56). At the same time the transformation in the production relations in agriculture meant that the nobility did not feel the same responsibility for the relief of their serfs. The national state was still in its early phases of development and was neither equipped nor inclined to take this responsibility. In this transitional period, social relief for the poor was provided through traditional organizations, such as guilds, extended family relations, communities and churches. The role of the religious body was particularly notable. "Monasteries, churches, hospitals and other institutions run by the church became the national network for relieving poverty" (George 1973:4).

This was the beginning of the development of the laissez-faire ideology, an ideology that divided politics from economics. To promote the "free markets" laborers had to be forced to sell their labor capacity for low wages. This would be possible only if relief remained substantially lower than subsistence level. Poverty was not considered to be a social problem; it was equated with laziness, the moral fault and subversive behavior of some individuals which had to be mercilessly repressed by the state. It was seen as equivalent to vagrancy, threatening the existing social order, requiring coercive and repressive measures by government. The fourteenth century Statute of Laborers is an example of this approach: "because that many valiant beggars, as long as they may live of begging, do refuse to labor, giving themselves to idleness and vice, and sometimes to theft and other abomination; it is ordained, that none, upon pain of imprisonment shall, under the colous of pity or alms, give anything to favor them toward their desires; so that thereby they may be compelled to labor for their necessary living" (Chambliss 1964:68). In order to force the dispossessed to labor at wages barely enough to cover their subsistence, even alms had to be prohibited and even the right to charity had to be denied. This is because charity, like other subsistence rights, was considered to be an alternative to wage labor.

The confiscation of the property of the church and monasteries by Henry VIII in the early part of the sixteenth century resulted in increased misery of the poor. This is because the church, the major relieving agency of the time, was impoverished. The result was a worsening of the situation of the poor for several decades until another agency, the local parish, was endowed with the responsibility to carry out the relief. To restrict the mobility of labor and vagrancy, the principle of "settlement" was adopted on the basis of which a person had a right to relief only in his own parish and in this way the basic responsibility for the poor from private charity and the church was transferred to parish offices (Marshall 1981:31).

III. The emergence and the development of social policy: The Poor Law period

The new national policy to regulate and direct the relief activities of the parish was incorporated in the Elizabethan Act of 1601. In spite of its repressive content, this act was a considerable advancement for the relief of the poverty of the working population. The question is why the monarchy decided to introduce less brutal measures for the relief of poverty. Jordan has stated, "it may safely be said that the steady concern of the Tudors with the problem of poverty from the almost obsessive preoccupation of these greater rulers with the question of public order" (Jordan 1959: 77). In his view the monarchy was "deeply persuaded that unrelieved and uncontrolled poverty was the most fertile breeding ground for local disasters which might be a kind of social contagion flame across the whole realm" (Ibid: 7). This notion is confirmed by Rimlinger: "in England, France and other European countries, governments became initially concerned with the lot of the poor not for purposes of relieving suffering, but for the maintenance of law and order" (Rimlinger 1971: 19).

Whether we agree with this assessment or not, the measures adopted in this act presented a considerable advancement in the development of welfare capitalism. The new institution, called poor relief, replaced the old charity by the church and the wealthy. Although it might have been adopted in order to maintain social harmony, it was administered strictly, strictly enough to force the laboring population from a disrupted subsistence economy into the labor market. The Act and the subsequent regulations and arrangements were set to prevent the use of relief by the laboring poor as a substitute for employment. As Piven and Cloward (1985) have stated, there were two main principles which guided the administration of relief programs in the Poor Laws period as well as in our own time. The first principle was to deny assistance to the able-bodied and employable, no matter whether any employment opportunity was in fact available. The second principle guided the policy makers to make conditions for the receipt of any assistance shameful enough to force the workers to accept the harshest types of work.

Marshall (1981) finds some positive elements in the Elizabethan Poor Law: "its case is strange because one finds so much in it that seems to anticipate the ideas and policies of a much later age" (p. 31). And he explains this positive aspect by stating that "the novel element was the fact that the Poor Laws were only one part of a remarkably comprehensive social and economic program, devised by the national government and executed by a centralized administrative machine of exceptional power and efficiency." In fact the national aspect of this new policy induced some level of regularity and uniformity which did not exist in the old system of charity and alms by individuals and the church and in a way would resemble the national and universal aspect of social rights developed about three centuries later. But the restrictive aspect of this Act has also been recognized by Marshall: "the problem envisaged by the government was not simply that of poverty, but of how to repair, revitalize and maintain a rationally conceived stratified social order, stable and static enough to enable everybody to find and keep his allotted place in it, while allowing scope for enterprise at the top and innovation on the fringes through chartered companies, monopolies and selective immigration." His assessment is consistent with a Marxian interpretation maintaining that the Poor Law measures (and the welfare state policies) were adopted by the state in order to retain social harmony and stability without endangering the tenets of the property system and the normal function of capital accumulation.

The Elizabethan Act with all its repressive measures was still superior to the New Poor Law Act of 1834 in which outdoor relief to the poor was abolished. For about two centuries the system built up by the Tudors remained more or less intact. During this period, which is usually referred to as "Elizabethan England," relief was dispensed to a good many people, usually in the restrictive form of outdoor relief. According to Dorothy Marshall, this covered "the greater part of the lower working class." In actuality not only the destitute but also a part of the working population who were at the margin of poverty were covered. The execution of the policies was in the hands of the overseers of the Poor Law whose task was to look after the welfare of the poor in matters of employment, education, health, housing and providing clothes, fuel and food in cases of urgency, and also giving allowances to poor laborers with large families (Dorothy Marshall 1926: 2,3). But as Marshall (1981: 32) has stated, the measures served to maintain the whole system of stratification and legitimate inequalities by law and administrative order. The relief policy was a part of a more comprehensive system which was set up to control the recruitment of each level of occupations to the appropriate class, imposing restrictions on mobility of the workers and fixing wages (at the minimum subsistence level).

The objective of the poor relief system was to keep outdoor relief as limited as possible. Apart from outdoor relief, three main methods were enforced by the parishes to ameliorate poverty: the workhouses, the Roundsman system and the Speenhamland system. In the sixteenth and seventeenth centuries indoor relief was very limited. It was after the Act of 1722 that the use of workhouses as a method of relief became more widespread. The shift from outdoor relief to the workhouse system was of course a set-back for the needy families. On the basis of the Act of 1722, the parish overseers were endowed with the authority to deny relief to the poor families if they refused to enter the workhouse. The conditions of life in the workhouse were harsh and the standard of living very low. The objective was to deter laborers from accepting relief and to drive them into the labor market, accepting the near starvation wages. In addition to this, workhouses were used by all age groups, for both sexes, and for the married and the single. In short, the use of workhouse relief was based on the philosophy of punishment and deterrence and it was confined to those desperate enough to accept the degradation attached to it.

In spite of the harshness of the workhouses, unemployment and poverty continued to increase. The pressure of unemployment was particularly acute in the rural areas due to economic changes in the eighteenth century. These changes were the intensified enclosure movement and the expansion of the cotton industry. The introduction of the factory mode of production resulted in the rapid rise in the supply of cotton and lower prices. The independent handloom weavers could neither compete with machines, nor with the low wages paid to women and children hired in an increasing number by the factory owners. These producers and the displaced agricultural workers, set free and dispossessed by the enclosure movement, were submerged in a more or less uniform class of "proletarian outworkers" (Thompson 1965: 271). Many of these displaced workers did not find employment in towns and as a result the number of the unemployed and the poor in rural areas increased. The use of the workhouses was not prevalent in rural areas and other measures had to be searched for. Hence the Roundsman and the Speenhamland systems were used, sometimes jointly and other times separately.

Webb had defined the Roundsman system as "a sort of billeting of the unemployed labor upon the parishowners in rotation, each in turn having to provide maintenance and being free to exact service" (cited in George 1973: 10). The Speenhamland system was developed on the basis of the magistrates at the Pelican Inn in Speenhamland, Berkshire to meet the situation in a rough and ready way by authorizing the Poor Law authorities to supplement the earnings of family men by amounts varying with the price of bread and the number of their children" (Sir John Walley 1972: 15).

The Speenhamland system was clearly favorable to the rich landowners who were still the ruling power group in the parishes, since the wages of the laborers were subsidized by taxes paid by all parishowners. It was at the same time a welcome respite from the harsh and degrading life of the workhouse for the working families. On the other hand, the operation of these systems was made possible "by the demand of the larger farmers in an industry which has exceptional requirements for occasional or causal labor- for a permanent cheap labor reserve" (Thompson 1968: 244).

During more than the two centuries between the Elizabethan Poor Law and the New Poor Law of 1834, the poor achieved some occasional victories in gaining relatively more liberal poor relief procedures. But in the longer run, they lost this struggle. The Act of 1834 was on the whole a set-back in the development of the welfare programs in Britain. With the passage of time the employers, both the industrialists and the landlords, were able to increase their control over the labor market and their influence on poor relief policies. While in the sixteenth century more than only a few workhouses did not exist, they increased in number and indoor relief grew in importance in subsequent centuries. In term of social welfare programs, this was a period of regression rather than progression.

IV. The transition from the Poor Law to the welfare state

The post-war introduction of the welfare state in Britain is generally acknowledged to have served as a model for other Western regimes (Briggs 1961). As Janowitz has observed, "In Great Britain the elaborate welfare state as a societal definition came into existence in one dramatic step with the election of the labor government in 1945" (1976: 39). But this sudden appearance of the "welfare state" in Britain was based on certain developments which began immediately after the New Poor Law was introduced by the Act of 1834. "The doctrine of the New Poor Law was that everyone must be given the strongest possible incentive to provide for the needs of himself and his family, not only while at work but in all the foreseen and unforeseen circumstances in which this would not be possible; and all this was to be done without state assistance" (Sir John Walley 1972: 27). This means that the introduction of the New Poor Law represented the absolute primacy of accumulation requirements over considerations for social needs. It was the culmination of the inherent principles of poor relief which had been resisted for several centuries by the poor. The strongest form of legitimation for the repressive measures incorporated in this law was provided by political economy through the doctrine of laissez faire. While the men of property had long supported measures to limit and even eliminate the rights of the laboring population to subsistence, never before had they been able to make such a strong case for a total rebuff of such rights.

Malthus' view that poor relief was a bounty on population was accepted as a basis of the Poor Law. The Poor Law Commission of 1834, considered the relief as a "bounty on indolence and vice". The influence of the conservative approach in political economy is evidenced by the fact that Nassau Senior, one of the most outspoken political economists, was the architect of the 1834 Poor Law (Friedman 1981: 48). It was the reflection of this view in the Poor Law Commission when it declared that "we do not believe that a country in which that distinction (the distinction between the recipient of relief and the independent laborers of the lowest class) has been completely effaced, and every man, whatever be his conduct or his character, ensured a comfortable subsistence, can retain its prosperity, or even its civilization" (cited in George 1975: 12).

But the "Poor Law" victory came rather late in history and the forces which eventually undermined it were already building. The voices of dissent were already heard from some followers of Ricardian theory who used it to derive a relatively different conclusion with respect to relief and welfare. In the 1830's Michael Sadler, Samuel Read, and Poulett Scrope presented strong contractarian cases for the fundamental rights of the poor to subsistence (Gilbert 1988: 154). In the New Poor Law of 1834, only the impotent and the destitute were eligible for relief. The right of the able-bodied poor to receive subsistence is best reflected in the following passage by Samuel Read:

> When, in the midst of a civilized society where the land is all appropriated, the division of labor established, and where no legal provision has been made for the poor, it happens to the laborer that he is unable to procure employment, and has nothing to eat, he is in effect commanded to starve without resistance, and without any effort to save himself. But what sanction has the society of which he is a member to offer, which should induce him to comply with so inhuman and so unreasonable a command?
>
> In the state of nature the land would still have remained open to him, and he would have been at full liberty to use all his exertions to procure subsistence; and whatever difficulty he might at times have found in acquiring his daily food, he never could have wanted employment. But in the advanced state of society before described the case is totally changed; to the unemployed laborer in that state the land is entirely locked up, his hands are tied, and he is placed in the cruellest of all situations, being expected and called upon (where no provision is made for his case) to perish for want in the midst of plenty. (Cited in Gilbert 1988: 155)

A more moderate defense of the right to subsistence and a progressive abandonment of the hard-line Malthusian doctrine on subsistence entitlement is reflected in the views of Mountfort Longfield and W.F. Lloyd, two noted economists of the time (Gilbert 1988: 158). In Longfield's assessment:

> The institution of society and the appropriation of landed property may be considered analogous to a bill for the

enclosure of a common, which in equity should give an adequate compensation to all who are thereby deprived of a right of commonage. The support of the destitute may be considered as the compensation for the right of commonage which they have lost by the regulations of society. (Cited in Gilbert 1988: 161)

A similar view is expressed by Lloyd who was a fellow of the Royal Society and the Drummond Professor of Political Economy at Oxford University:

The proposition that, in a world already possessed, none whose labor is not wanted have any claim of right to the smallest portion of food, involves a monstrous consequence. It implies that the right of the possessors of the world to do with it as they please, though they may not amount to a thousandth part of the population, are yet at liberty to say to the rest, 'we have no need of you: we will raise up a new generation to execute our pleasure. (Cited in Gilbert 1988: 161)

In spite of such objections to Malthusian notions of relief and the measures incorporated in the Act of 1834, the actual transition from the Poor Law began no sooner than the first decade of the twentieth century. The pace of social change was this time considerably faster. While it took more than three centuries for the main principles of the Poor Law system to be firmly established, the transition from the Poor Law to a modern version of the welfare state took less than one century. The Industrial Revolution and rising productivity and changes in technology had induced a faster pace of socioeconomic changes in society.

The first important legislation for social programs occurred in Britain in 1908. The Pension Act of 1908 has been singled out by Heclo (1974) as a landmark departure from the mentality of the Poor Law. He maintains that prior to this act "the citizens claim to state support rested upon either the performance of specific services as in the military or civil services, or the submission to disqualifying restrictions in return for general public aid. Old age pensioners were the first significant portion of the population able to gain entitlement to state support by virtue of being citizens requiring such and without any effect upon their status as members of the community" (1974: 156). But while this act was a considerable advancement, it retained some of the stigma of the old poor relief.

The payment of pension in this act was made conditional upon an income test and certain moral clauses. Thus those whose incomes exceeded a stipulated maximum did not receive any pension; those whose income was below a minimum received the full amount of pension, and those whose income was in between received a part of the full pension. There were also included in this Act a number of moral clauses disqualifying those who had not worked regularly or had been convicted of drunkenness, etc. (George 1973: 17).

A more comprehensive legislation was the National Insurance Act of 1911. This was the first universal national insurance Act in Western countries. In this Act, people at work were required to pay contributions. Employers and the state had also to contribute to the fund which financed the benefits. Most manual workers in case of illness but only a small section of the unemployed were covered by this Act. Two institutions of insurance and the labor exchange were combined in this Act (Friedman 1981: 70). Beveridge has stated, "The state is forced into the costly and degrading harshness of the Poor Law simply because it has no control or supervision of the labor market. It must rely always on the assumption that the applicant for help could find work if he looked for it because it is never in the position to satisfy itself that there is not work for him" (cited in Friedman 1981: 70). Beveridge's device to solve this problem had two components. First, the workers had to register at the employment exchange to establish that they were looking for a job. Second, they had an earned right to benefit on the basis of past contributions (Ibid: 70). In this way, the new insurance system could be consistent with the principle of self-help. On the basis of this principle, workers would make savings that could be used as insurance for a future time. In fact the degrading aspect of the Poor Law forced many workers to take out an insurance policy with friendly societies or trade unions (George 1973: 18). From here there was one step further to replace this form of private insurance by a universal compulsory system run by the state.

The question to be addressed now is: What caused this transformation of social policy by the turn of the century? The reasons for this change are diverse and different authors have proposed various explanations. The introduction and evolution of social insurance systems in Western countries might be interpreted as a kind of diffusion process. This model is suggested by Reinhard Bendix who explains it as a process of modernization: "basic element of modernization is that it refers to a type of social change since the eighteenth century, which consists in the economic and political advance of some pioneering society and the subsequent changes in the follower societies" (Bendix 1967: 331). The pioneering society is Germany under Bismarck in which the first large-scale social insurance schemes were introduced in 1880's.

This hypothesis has been supported by Asa Briggs who has attributed future welfare legislation to the German initiative: "German social insurance stimulated foreign imitation. Denmark, for example, copied all three German pension schemes between 1891 and 1898" (Briggs 1961: 147).

Collier and Messick, in their study of the diffusion process in Western Europe, come to the conclusion that internal socioeconomic conditions played little role in the initial introduction of social security legislation. In their view the introduction of such programs from 1883 to 1907 was the result of a diffusion process "up a hierarchy of nations" from the less to the most developed societies. They argue that the follower societies adopted social insurance programs at consistently higher levels of political mobilization and at a higher or at least the same level of socioeconomic development (Collier and Messick, 1975, Flora and Alber 1982, and Kuhnle 1982).

As Flora and Alber (1982) have stated, "Although diffusion processes may have affected the course of national decision making, the example set by pioneer country does not apparently provide sufficient incentive to adopt social insurance schemes independent of internal socioeconomic problems and political mobilization" (p.63). It is reasonable to assume that if Germany had not initiated social insurance programs, another country might have innovated them somewhat later. In such a case, the pattern of initial development, of social programs could have been, to a certain extent, different.

V. The Keynesian welfare state and its post-war development

During World War II the working class in Britain was taken into a corporatist relationship, with civil liberties restricted because of war needs. The conditions of war led to a sort of central control and created many state structures with corporatist tendencies. The need for coordinating production and interests of employers and employees provided a foundation for corporatist structure. The industrial concord which was established gave certain material gains to workers in exchange for a number of restrictions on their activities. The workers lost their right to strike and to move freely from one industry to another. In return, the employers had to hire labor only via trade unions or official labor exchanges. A strict control on prices was to be adopted by the Treasury, and in return wage demands had to be limited. In this period, the Ministry of Labor acquired a powerful position in coordinating the relationship between labor and capital. A joint consultative committee was established which brought the union leadership into government on a consultancy basis with equal representation to that of employers. For the purpose of joint consultation between employers and unions at regional levels, joint production committees were set up (Scott, 1982).

The main component of the industrial strategy and war effort in the Second World War was a manpower policy. The need for labor as the major resource to win the war provided the Trades Union Congress with a more advantageous position. In this period, real wages increased and the income of workers rose rapidly because of long overtime. At the same time salaries declined by 21 percent in the 1938-47 period, and income from property fell by 15 percent (Scott, 1982).

Part of the political concordat of the war period was a trade in which workers sacrificed during the war in return for social reform after the war. After a major victory in the 1945 elections, the newly elected labor government proceeded to implement a social democratic program based on Keynesian macroeoconomic policy and on the extension and consolidation of a welfare state. Internally Keynesianism took over, but Britain's external policy was governed by the perspectives of liberal political economy. Keynesianism justified a state role in the economy and rejected the orthodox notion that the government should not concern itself with the overall performance of the economy. But in principles "It remained compatible with the goals of liberal political economy, because it proposed no interference with the detailed workings of markets and individual decision-making, only with aggregate demand, aggregate investment, and national income". (A.Gamble, 1981: 144).

The post-war economic and social programs had the support of not only the Trade Union Congress (TUC), but also the approval of the Federation of British Industries (FBI) which was the main organization representing the interests of industry (Jessop, 1980). In the war period, the trade unions and employers associations were elevated from interest groups to governing institutions. "Equilibrium was maintained because the governing institutions came to share some of the political power and attributes of the state itself avid to admit bodies to its orbit rather than face-for-all with a host of individual claimants" (Middlemas 1979: 20)-Mobilizing civil servants around the national interest slogan, the war-time government gave a share to labor, industry, and the City in governing the economy. In fact, the labor movement, as an integral part of the development of the political economy of capitalism, is linked with the development of state welfare. The demands put forward by the labor organizations played an important role for social legislation to improve the life chances of working people. In comparing Britain with the U.S., we will notice that the labor organizations were influential in forcing the state to be responsible for basic needs.

The post-war settlement facilitated a shift from the corporatism of the war period to a Keynesian welfare state. In fact both Keynes and Beveridge were influential in the formulation of the post-war policies of economic and social intervention by the state. The state committed itself to a policy of full employment and economic stability by applying the Keynesian policy of demand management, and at the same time the reform in social security and the extension of the welfare programs in line with the Beveridge Report (Flora and Heidenheimer, 1982). The demands of labor were reformist and aimed at immediate material gains rather than a radical transformation of society. The wartime planning apparatus was dismantled and the joint consultative committee briefly lost its actual power (Jessop, 1980).

The three main institutions of the modern welfare state in Britain, National Assistance, the reformed National Insurance Act, and the National Health Service, were all introduced in 1948. National assistance was later replaced by "Supplementary Benefits" which allowed the extension of the range of benefits covering additional subsidies, such as rent and rate rebates, fuel allowances, clothing grants, etc. (Jessop, 1980). In contrast to the Poor Law benefits, the emphasis of the new programs was on a universal "national minimum" to which every citizen was entitled. The Poor Law confined public relief outside the workhouse to the infirm.

In the new policy, certain benefits, such as unemployment insurance, applied just to the able-bodied. To qualify for such benefits, the unemployed were only obliged to be willing to accept those jobs which were suitable in light of their previous employment. This approach was substantially different from the Poor Law which was concerned primarily with the maintenance of the labor market and forcing the poor to accept any employment at whatever wage (Piven and Cloward, 1985: Chapter 2). Of course, the new system was also concerned with maintaining the work ethic and regulating the poor. It adopted measures to separate the able-bodied unemployed from the socially declassed poor through differentiated protection schemes. The differentiation and fragmentation of the benefits, in turn, intensified the already existing fragmentation of the working population and would generate struggles over welfare rights among various claimant groups. The subsequent developments in measures related to so-called "fiscal welfare", such as tax concessions and subsidies for private welfare provisions in areas such as pensions, housing, life insurance, and child care, exacerbated the inherent fragmentation and polarization tendency of the system (Jessop, 1980).

The rising involvement of the state in different aspects of social and economic life of society led to the characteristic increase in public expenditures which we may observe in all advanced capitalist countries in the post-war period. Public expenditures as a percentage of GNP increased from around 30 percent in 1950 to 46 percent in 1975 (OECD, 1976). The rapid economic growth of the recovery period enabled Britain and other Western countries to expand their public expenditures in all fields. To understand the implication of this trend for the expansion of the welfare state and social policy, one has to differentiate between various components of public spending to find out which grow most rapidly and thereby dominate the overall increase. Studies on the welfare state have normally concentrated on either social transfer items or social expenditures as the main indicators for the growth of the welfare state and have tended to neglect the contribution of other state expenditures in the standards of living of the working population. Social transfer payments may be considered as publicly supported private consumption, since they contribute to the consumption of market goods. These expenditures in the U.K. increased from 5.7 percent of the GNP in 1950 to above 11 percent in 1975 (OECD, 1976). This is a significant increase. But even in 1975, social transfer expenditures did not constitute a large share of national output. Other European countries allocated more resources toward these expenditures. This is specially true in the case of France, Italy and the Netherlands in which social transfer expenditures as a proportion of GNP were 20 percent or more in 1975 (OECD, 1976). But this item, by itself, is not an adequate indicator of the welfare state growth.

Another alternative is to measure total social expenditures, defined as all expenditures for social risk and need, irrespective of the mode of payment (i.e., cash or in kind.) This is a broader concept of social expenses than social transfer payments. In addition to transfer payments, social expenditures also include certain public consumption and public investment expenditures. In the United Kingdom, social expenditures constituted 19.2 percent of GDP in 1975. Once again, this is one of the lowest levels among European nations (OECD, 1976). But this does not imply that the welfare policies and redistributive activities of the state in Britain are less developed than other members of EEC. Judging by total expenditures on social goods, as opposed to just social expenditures, Britain ranks as an average spender. The working population receives benefits not only from social expenditures but also from a number of other items, such as transportation, communication, and public utilities. These are the social goods which are not provided as a direct means of social policy. Up to the late 1970's, the share of the state budget spent on social goods has been higher than a number of other EEC members, such as France, Italy, and the Netherlands. However, in the recent decade, the share of social transfer expenses in total state expenditures considerably increased. This disproportionate growth of social transfer payments is primarily caused by the persistent high level of unemployment and the slippage of a larger proportion of the population into poverty.

The expansion of publicly provided goods and services associated with the welfare state required a relatively stable and growing economy. Beside the expansion of social welfare programs, the post-war settlement included the introduction of macro-level demand management and the commitment of the state to full-employment. This was of course part of the economic and political post-war accord between capital and labor. But it was also a necessary basis for the expansion of the welfare programs. A substantial decline in economic activity and a significant increase in the level of unemployment, as is now well known, would have resulted in the fiscal crisis of the state. There was in this way a necessary relationship between these two components of "the Keynesian welfare state". Within the context of the strong post-war economic recovery with fairly stable and relatively high rates of economic growth, low unemployment, and low inflation, it seemed safe to assume that Keynesian policy was itself the principal cause of this unprecedented prosperity. But this belief has been challenged recently by Tomlinson (1981) who argued that there never was a Keynesian policy in Britain, and such a policy could not have been adopted under the circumstances of the post-war period. Thus, the economic recovery of the post-war period had to be explained in a different way. In his view, the almost full employment economy of the 1950's and 1960's was caused by an autonomous private investment boom. He further argues that constraints on policy, particularly the internal and external constraints on public borrowing, did not permit the government to adopt an expansionary deficit spending policy even if it had wanted to.

A counter-argument has been put forward by Scott (1982), who suggests that government policy has tended to encourage private investment. He also argues that Keynesian policy, at least in the Neo-Classical synthesis form, has been applied in Britain. The fact that this policy was not expansionary at all times is explained by the fact that booms and inflationary trends required occasional anti-inflationary measures. Scott agrees that the post-war boom was primarily initiated by rising private investment, but argues that the state would have intervened to stimulate the economy if and to the degree that economic conditions had required it.

Both these arguments are limited by the fact that they address the application of Keynesian policy from a rather narrow and technical perspective. The state can not be characterized as a unified entity with a single will, responding to the economic requirement of stability in a rational and neutral manner. It seems reasonable to argue that Keynesian policy was not the primary cause of the post-war economic boom. The strategy of the 1960's was consistent with the Keynesian presumption. But the assumption of Keynsianism was not in line with liberal political economy that market obstacles should be removed. (Rodney Lowe, 1993, p. 16). On the other hand, the expansionary and anti-inflationary policies adopted were not determined primarily by economic circumstances. As Caves et al, 1968 have suggested, the timing of policies often served to reinforce, rather than reduce, the effect of cyclical fluctuations on investment and output. The pattern of macroeconomic policy in Britain can be best characterized as the recurrence of a "stop-go" cycle. This means that government policy was a continual oscillation between inflation and often sharp deflation (Hall, 1983). Government policy can be better understood by analyzing the socioeconomic organization of British society.

The most important feature of the organization of capital in Britain has been the separation of financial and industrial capital and the relative hegemony of the former in public decision-making and economic policy. The institution representing the interests of financial capital, the Bank of England, has been endowed with considerable autonomy and has been able to exercise substantial influence in shaping economic policy (Jessop, 1980). Industrial capital, on the other hand, has been much more fragmented and does not enjoy the same level of concentration, and centralization as financial capital does. The main business organizations, the Federation of British Industry and the British Employers' Confederation have not been able to coordinate the activities of different fractions of industrial capital. In contrast with financial capital, there has not been any particular state institution to promote the interests of industrial capital in any consistent way (Hall, 1983). The main organization of labor, Trades Union Congress, is a loose confederation with limited resources and limited authority over its members. While the labor organizations have been relatively strong at shop-floor level, the lack of a centralized union system has prevented the workers from exercising any substantial influence on economic policy (Jessop, 1980).

The "stop-go" pattern of macroeconomic policy can be understood within this framework. The government often adopted expansionary policy during the "go" phase of these cycles to induce employment and economic growth. The absence of any institutions within the state to represent and further the interests of industrial capital and labor, and the substantial influence of the Bank of England supporting the interests of the financial capital on matters of economic policy, frequently resulted in the stop phase or reversal of expansionary measures adopted to stimulate economic activity. Given the high degree of the British economy's exposure to international flows of commodities and capital, such measures resulted in increased imports and the deterioration of the balance of payment. To address this problem, the British policy makers had to devalue the currency or to deflate the economy. They often opted for the second. The pressure of the finance capital articulated by the Bank of England, and the desire to maintain the strength of the pound as a major international currency and the City as a powerful financial center, pressed the government to adopt deflationary policies in almost all these cases (Hall, 1983). The consistent defense of the exchange rate implied a seriously overvalued currency having adverse effect on industrial production (Brittan, 1971: pp. 298-9).

In light of this analysis, it would be fair to say that the British government more often adopted Keynesian macroeconomic measures halfheartedly. This is not to suggest that any full and rational application of Keynesian policy would have prevented the relative decline of the British economy or the crisis of the 1970's. The British economy was facing structural problems and these types of macroeconomic measures would not have been suitable or at least adequate in addressing such problems. The expansionary macroeconomic policies had to be adopted in conjunction with an activist industrial policy. But this aspect remained a neglected feature of policy making until the 1960's. It was during this period that attempts were made to adopt measures of industrial policy and engage in a certain degree of economic planning (Hall, 1986). But as this analysis regarding the organizational relationship between the state, capital and labor reveals, the institutional framework was inadequate to the task of achieving tripartite agreements among the major players in the economy.

It should be sufficient here, without going into any further detail, to mention that the state's attempt in developing such institutions and pursueing a widespread industrial policy has remained largely unsuccessful. However, this trend resulted in a gradual development of an approach which we may call "quasi-corporatist." As a result of these developments, a number of para-state institutions, such as the National Economic Development Council (NEDC or "Neddy"), the Industrial Reorganization Corporation, and the National Enterprise Board emerged during the 1960's and 1970's with the purpose of restructuring industrial capital and promoting the advancement of technology and productivity (Hall, 1986). But still the Treasury and the Bank have been able to retain substantial control over short-term economic policy, prohibiting the state from pursuing a consistent long-term policy of industrial restructuring which is required for British industry to become internationally competitive. This pattern of state intervention and inability of the state to achieve consensus between capital and labor and to reorganize industrial production, has enhanced the emergence of a large number of quasi-government organizations (or quagos) and "quasi-non government organizations" (or quangos) with a considerable degree of independence. The proliferation of quagos and quangos has extended bureaucratic domination over the economy and policy and has reduced the influence of elected officials and parliament in control over policies (Jessop, 1980). This process has certainly facilitated the shift towards "authoritarian populism" and favorable climate for the growing influence of neo-conservatism and the rise of Thatcherism. Monetarism became part of a broader ideological and political attack upon government intervention and upon social democracy. The monetarist doctrines became influential over the controlling of inflation, state intervention, a step backward toward the orthodox policy.

Thatcherism was associated with a commitment to restore competition and personal responsibility for effort and reward. It was an attack on the "big state," based on the promise of rolling back the frontiers of the state and drastically cutting taxes and expenditures to enhance economic revival, and extending the domain of individual choice and freedom. Thatcherism emerged as the leading ideological force to revitalize conservatism. It did not abandon the old Keynesian demand management policies. Thatcherism's anti-statism by the deregulation of the financial market, the attack on public employment in both local and central government, and the destruction of quagos tried to dismantle corporatist structure (McCrone 1988: 57). It was a project "to reverse the post-war Keynesian welfare-corporatist consensus" (Britten, 1985: 52). The state has intervened directly to undermine the power of organized labor and "it extended its powers over local government through rate-capping" (McCrone 1988: 58).

The Thatcher government adopted a new method for regulating public expenditure and money supply by applying monetarism rigidly to control inflation. In actual practice the movement towards a stronger state and increased authoritarianism continued and was even intensified. But the attempt of the government to slash public expenditures and reduce the budget deficit was never successful. There certainly was a cut-back in certain welfare expenditures and a slow-down in the growth of other social programs. The government tried to control public spending through a tax cut policy but at the same time it increased spending on defense, law, and order. The rise in general state expenditures was 13.6 percent in real terms between 1979 and 1987 (HMSO, 1987). Thatcher's government was careful not to privatize the health, welfare, and education services. As a result, notwithstanding its target to cut the budget deficit and public debt, its borrowing requirement remained large, interest rates were pushed up by the financial markets, company profits were squeezed and the unemployment rate went up. The increase in unemployment rate and the spread of poverty to a larger number of families resulted in the rise of the total value of welfare expenditures (see Chapter six in this book). The increase in defense outlays, the cost of supporting bankrupt industries, and the insistence of the government on not increasing taxes exacerbated the budget deficit. By the end of 1980 the government faced a new recession. With a high level of unemployment (two million), a high level of inflation rate, government strategy was in deep trouble. Because Thatcherism did not seek to improve the existing pattern of inequality, it did generate increasing opposition among a wide range of groups; "women activists, anti-nuclear movements, tax payers' revolts, gay rights organizations, and political agitation by immigrant and by discontented youth" (Krieger 1986: 187).

2 The literature on economic boundaries of the welfare state: The legitimacy of the welfare state and economic growth

I. The liberal legitimation

The liberal legitimation of the welfare state has been associated with a functionalist approach toward the role of the state in society. The market system was seen as unable to perform certain necessary functions required for economic and social stability. The role of the state was, then, to correct for the imperfections of the market mechanism. In sociology, Parsons, Smelser, and other social scientists developed a theory of functional relationship between different parts of society. It is argued that the development of state welfare institutions has been the result of this functional necessity and structural differentiation. "Development gives birth to dozens of institutions and organizations geared to these new integrative problems-labor recruitment agencies and exchanges, labor unions, government relation of labor allocation, welfare and relief arrangements, co-operation societies, and savings institutions" (Smelser 1964: 268). With the development of the industrial society, institutional specialization develops further. As a result of this the extended family and the local community weaken as collectivities and religious organizations weaken in acting as integrative institutions. The role of these social institutions is to provide harmony and integration among different parts of society.

The welfare institution, according to this view, belongs to the integrative sub-system. They believe in two kinds of integration: system integration (the integration of institutions) which is concerned with the instrumental aspects of the collectivity and social integration (integration of social groups). Their importance is because of their contribution towards efficiency, stability and order. For them social welfare institutions are seen as a consequence of the need of a community for solidarity among constituting groups and the recognition of the individuals' needs in the community to replace the model of family and kinship institutions in pre-industrial societies. "Whereas the problem of social integration focuses attention upon the orderly or conflict relationship between the actors, the problem of system integration focuses on the orderly or conflictful relationship between the parts, of a social system" (Lockwood 1964: 244-56). Here the focus of attention is on the problem of conflict between groups. The society is seen as analogous to an organism. The function of social institutions must be performed to serve a society. The functional division of labor among the institutions of society has been analyzed as a necessity for good fit or harmony. Functional inconsistency among the parts of an integrated system is the source of conflict among various social groups and change.

In contrast with Marxian theory in which the contradiction between the forces of production and the relations of production is the basis of social change, in this view group conflict is the fundamental source of social change. In Lockwood's words, "one might almost say that the conflict which in Marxian theory is decisive for change is not the power conflict arising from the relationships in the productive system, but the system conflict arising from contradiction between the property institutions and the forces of production" (Lockwood 1964: 250). This approach would then recognize the possibility of disequilibrium and dysfunction in society. This would, however, be a transitory situation and the evolution of the required institutions would return equilibrium and harmony to the society. This notion of social integration is in line with Durkheim's view that the complexity of the modern society requires co-ordination and regulation. Durkheim notes the state as the central organ of society. "A multitude of functions which where diffuse become concentrated. The care of educating the young, of protecting public health, of presiding over the ways of administering public aid, of administering the means of transport and communication, little by little move over into the sphere of the central organ" (Cited in Mishra 1981: 52). For him this increasing integrative role of government organs has been an evolutionary development in response to the disintegrating impact of market development and industrialization.

A similar functionalist approach toward the role of the state can also be seen in the theory of the "industrial society" (Mishra 1984). In this approach, social policy is seen as social engineering. The advanced Western societies are characterized as industrial or post-capitalist societies which are neither capitalist nor socialist. Economic and social intervention by the state is considered to be functionally necessary for such a society (Mishra 1981: chap. 3). In "convergence theory" the role of industrialization is considered to be very crucial in establishing welfare institutions. The industrial characteristics of modern societies are influential structural patterns in shaping the institutions of welfare and in functionally integrating the social structure. In this doctrine the determinant factor is technology and not class structure and not political affiliation (see Kerr et al., 1973,. Galbraith 1967, Mishra 1981). It is assumed that all advanced industrial societies move towards a similar institutional economy and social structure.

It is thus argued that the state in the institutional pattern of welfare accepts the responsibility of meeting needs instead of friendly societies, charities, voluntary organizations, co-operatives of an earlier age. Industrial societies give the state the responsibility "for guaranteeing the minimum welfare and security of industrial man" (Kerr et al., 1973: 186). In such an advanced society, state and the enterprise organising production to maintain an efficient work force. In this process of industrialization welfare institutions are transformed from a residual type to an institutional one. Industrial societies are seen as atomistic organizations in which state intervention is minimal and distribution of resources are fulfilled through the market system.

In this approach, market-based distribution is regulated by the state in recognition of need. In the early stages of industrialization state welfare is assumed to be residual and is limited to a small portion of the population which takes the form of poor relief. In an advanced industrial society state welfare takes a form between the residual model and the normative one. In this approach, the ideological nature and the class content of the state activities are disregarded and economic policy and social policy are seen in a technical perspective, more like management of things rather than coordination of economic and social relations. Their notion of welfare is one-sided looking at society as a whole without paying attention to the effect of functions for the parts. As Mishra argued, social policies have different consequences on different groups and institutions that make the whole society. "Once the unitary view of society is abandoned, the concept of function becomes almost redundant" (Mishra 1981: 60). Any kind of society within its unity characteristics is made of diverse groups with diverse interests and conflicts and values. On the other hand, this view does not make a distinction between structures of welfare in different industrial societies. As far as integration is concerned, there is not a great difference between the Victorian Poor Law and more advanced welfare. The proponents of "Convergence Theory" see the development of welfare as a multiplication of roles and organization. The development of social policy is not only a reflection of a higher level of specialization. It is connected with the changes in value and income, and other demands of the members of society through the development of human processes.

The Neo-Classical theory of Public Economics is in certain respects in line with the above sociological theories. The Neo-Classical theory also adopts a functionalist approach towards the role of the state in society. The framework of the analysis is based on an ideal situation which is called Pareto optimal. Musgrave writes, "Our normative model of public economy is not designed to be realistic in the sense of describing what goes on in the capitals of the world. Rather, it is designed to show what would go on if an optimal result were achieved" (Musgrave, Public Finance, ch. 1). The optimality is attributed to an equilibrium position which is outcome of the competitive market forces. Since in reality there are many situations in which competitive forces are not in operation, the outcome may be less than optimum. Thus, in line with the above approaches, the market society is seen as imperfect and incomplete without state intervention. The state is essential to the functioning of a modern market economy on the basis of the norm of Pareto optimality, the core concept of welfare economics. The activities of the state are considered to be functionally necessary to correct for imperfections in the free market system. The failure of the market to perform certain required functions would lead to the intervention of the state (Musgrave-Musgrave 1984: Chapter 3 and Atkinson-Stiglitz 1980: Chapters 10, 11).

Hence government intervention, in this approach, should be partial, targeted at certain areas of non-optimality and market failures. But, in fact, the whole market economy would have failed without the existence of the state. Without state intervention to provide an external framework for exchange and accumulation, the whole market economy would not have operated. Stiglitz has acknowledged this by stating that "it is not really being assumed that the hypothetical free market situation could be attained in the absence of the government. There is indeed little reason to believe that the market could function in the way assumed in the "no-government economy" (Stiglitz 1981: 8). But this concept of market failure, i.e., the failure of the whole market system with a no state situation, is something which is not generally recognized by Neoclassical economists, and when recognized is not incorporated into their theory of the state. There are two aspects of this overall failure of the market system.

The first one is the failure of the capitalist market system in the absence of the role of the state in providing the external framework for accumulation and market transactions. The very system of property relations and the enforcement of contracts require the state provision of a judiciary system, its guarantee of a uniform and national form of money, etc. On the other hand, state activities are required to provide some extra-market form of subsistence, since in a capitalist economy the ability of workers to acquire subsistence depends on their success to find employment which is not guaranteed. But the amount of subsistence should not exceed beyond a certain level since it then may undermine the operation of the labor market. State involvement is therefore necessary to control and regulate the exchange of labor power. This means that the labor market can not operate without state intervention.

The second aspect of a total market failure has to do with the macro level movements of the market economy. Since the capitalist economy is crisis prone, there is always the possibility for an overall decline or even the collapse of market activities. This aspect of the overall market failure is acknowledged by Keynesian theory which incorporates certain interpretations of the instability of the market economy. Within this approach, the capitalist economy is perceived to be inherently unstable; the solution is considered to be some form of economic policy. This means that the role of the Keynesian state goes beyond its functional role in the provision of social goods and its activities to address the situations in which optimality is undermined. The Keynesian approach recognizes another function for the state and that is the provision of economic stability. In this way, economic policy, provision of public goods, and social policy are seen as the response of government to the failure of the market to perform such activities in an efficient way.

In all the above theories, the productive system of capitalism is taken as for granted. The State is considered to be neutral, responding to needs of all sections of society. They also share the belief in the ability of the state to manage economic and social affairs rationally. The notion of the rationalism of state intervention is also shared by Social Democrats who see social policy and piecemeal social engineering as a means for gradual movement of the society toward socialism.

II. The neo-conservative challenge

Keynesian economists had long assumed that the state could regulate the economy in response to the needs of society. The conservatives, on the other hand, argue that government involvement in economic and social affairs of society would only distort the operation of an otherwise efficient and responsive market system. Government failure is the central theme in the Neo-Conservative doctrine of the post-war state. Their argument is against the collectivist view of Keynes and Beveridge who believed that state agencies acted in a neutral way to identify public interest. Conservatives, with their common ground of methodological individualism, attack the rationality of state action. It is argued that because of the complexity of the process of social policy, the government may be serving private interest in the name of public interest. This has been seen as an invisible hand in the public sector. Friedman has stated that "in the government sphere, as in the market, there seems to be an invisible hand, but it operates in precisely the opposite direction from Adam Smith's ... government intervention is led by an invisible hand to promote private interest" (Friedman and Friedman 1980: 24). Hayek (1978) and Friedman (1977), among others, have emphasized their faith in the free market, i.e., the classical doctrines of the market and individualism. Hayek in defending the market system identifies it as "a communications system which we call the market and which turns out to be a more efficient mechanism for digesting dispersed information than any that man has deliberately designed" (Hayek 1978: 34). He rejects the functional forms of technological or sociological determinism which stimulate the necessity for big government. For Friedman "evidence that markets are imperfect does not create a case for government action which may be even more imperfect" (Friedman 1977: 7).

For the New Right the market system, as a kind of social institution which has been developed over the centuries as a result of interaction of large number of individuals, is superior as a means of coordinating to state direction. Wildavsky observes that "we may be smart; but life is smarter," i.e., the market is smarter (Wildavsky 1980: 21). In their view, only market forces could bring about the efficiency and competitiveness of the economy and they use this argument to attack the corporatist form of state intervention which they consider to be responsible for the malfunctioning of the economy. In the area of welfare, the conservatives tend towards a residual concept of welfare. This residual doctrine of welfare believes in the role of the state as relieving the hard core of poverty. In their view, Keynesian social policy would result in an overexpansion of the government, which they consider as the principal cause of the economic slow-down and rising inflation of the 1970's (Buchanan-Flowers 1980: chap. 6).

In fact, Britain is often used as an example in the argument that the expansion of state expenditures contributes to economic decline, inducing stagnation rather than innovation (Mishra 1984: chap. 2). When in the 1950's Britain was falling behind its competitors, critics blamed tripartism. The Right was disturbed as they saw that labor had become a governing institution and part of the ruling apparatus. From 1974 we have witnessed an emergence of organizations calling themselves the New Right. The second half of the 1970's was the period of success of the New Right movement. Large, small business, corporate leaders, and self-employed entrepreneurs complained about new legislation and high inflation rate, and overtaxation. They saw themselves under the burden of the labor laws.

The New Right considered unemployment as a natural feature of the market system which should have been seen as the price for growth and freedom in the economy, as a necessary factor of the free market economy because maintaining full employment artificially and externally to the internal laws of the market system would result in inflation. The policy of full employment by the government would harm the efficient natural laws of the market economy. In actuality the inflation rate rose to an unprecedented level in Britain. It was 16 per cent in 1974, 24.2 percent in 1975, 16.5 percent in 1976, and 15.9 percent in 1977. In the early 1970's company profits collapsed from about 8 percent per annum to less than 3 percent by the end of the decade (Useem 1983).

As a result , the "Neo-Liberals" emerged as the dominant factor during this decade to focus on setting the market free. Another trend was the conservative ideological strand in this emerging New Right. Their emphasis was to impose tighter social and moral discipline on society.

The liberals were interested not in a market economy but a market order. What they really wanted was a network of exchanges between different markets. The useful function of the state in this conjunction was to protect the fragile market order. Their attention was on the distributive role of government when individuals followed their self-interest in the political market.

The New Right, on the other hand, argue that this could cause a burden on the government and state could lose its capacity to manage effectively and corporatism was considered to be the result. From 1974 to 1975 Britain witnessed the creation of new organizations representing small businesses: National Federation For the Self-Employed (NFSE), Association of Self-Employed People (ASO), National Association of the Self-Employed (NASE), Independent Business Person's Association (IBPA) (McCrone 1988:51).

The revival of the Right is not simply the return to the old doctrine of individualism and laissez faire. They have put forward certain new ideas regarding the mechanism of state activities and their implications for the economy. They have tried to formulate certain theories to explain the current crisis. Their theoretical arguments have some remarkable resemblances to the view put forward by some Marxian theorists on the structural crisis of the state. Their views are however different from the left in addressing policy issues. For them the source of crisis is not the conditions of wage labor, but the institutional arrangements of the welfare state and mass democracy.

The conservatives, in general, consider the overexpansion of state activities as the source of the current crisis and the decline of the British economy. The overexpansion is associated with the pattern in which democratic rights are exercised. There are four aspects of the overexpansion of the state which are considered to have caused such problems. The first aspect is what has been called the crisis of ungovernability.

For the Neo-Conservatives the Western democratic state is faced with increasing demands by various organized interest groups and by the electorate. At the same time the process of democratization restricts government's authority and freedom to act efficiently. This contradictory development of the state has been referred to as the ungovernability of the liberal democratic state. Anthony King's view on the thesis of ungovernability is that "Britain has become harder to govern. The reason it has become harder to govern is that, at one and the same time, the range of problems that government is expected to deal with has vastly increased, and its capacity to deal with problems, even many of the ones it had before, has decreased. It is not the increase in the number of problems alone that matters, or the reduction in capacity. It is the two coming together (1976: 25). His solution for this overload problem is as follow: "governments have tried to play God. They have failed. But they go on trying. How can they be made to stop? Perhaps over the next few years, they should be more concerned with how the number of tasks that government has come to be expected to perform can be reduced" (1976: 26).

This state overload concept became a common belief among many of the Neo-Conservative critics of liberal democracies in the 1970's to protect markets from the threat of democracy. The policies which Conservatives came up with were influenced by monetarism organiated by Milton Friedman and the Chicago School; the idea that tight monetary policy will defeat inflation, one of the major economic problems of the 1970's. Monetarism was "the battering ram that made the breach" (Gamble 1986: 32) in the walls of Keynesianism and social democracy. What Hayek wanted was more than simply adopting the monetarist models, his desire was an attack on corporatism to free the market. His aim was to shrink trade union power by removing them from governmental institutions and by removing legal immunities, forcing labor to support the market rules. The adopted strategies of the elected conservative government of 1979 in Britain were to attack public spending and to cut taxation: a supply-side economics strategy. This doctrine asks the state to play the role of ensuring the market freedom to work and enforcing laws of contract. The aim was not the disappearance of the state "It is possible to use the state strategically to divest the state. The idea that 'New-Liberalism' meant the abolition rather than the decomposition of the state was always an illusion" (Hall 1986: 15).

The second argument is put forward in the work of Bacon and Eltis (1976), one of the most influential studies in this regard, in which the authors have considered the overexpansion of the state sector as the main factor contributing to the economic decline of Britain. They argue that the expansion of the government sector has diverted the resources from productive uses in the private sector. In their perspective, state activities are perceived as unproductive and wasteful and expanding government expenditures result in inefficiency and lower productivity. This argument is based on the notion that all government activities are unproductive while all economic activities in the private sector are inherently productive. The authors suggesting this analysis do not develop any clear distinction between productive and unproductive activities in the private sector.

Other studies such as Jones (1978) and Joseph (1976) have paid more attention to transfer payments and welfare expenditures. In these works, this aspect of public expenditures are held responsible for economic slow-down through their adverse effects on incentives of business to invest and workers to work. Another aspect of public expenditures determined to impair the growth of the economy is expanded public borrowing. This is the so-called "crowding out" effect of public borrowing. The increasing borrowing requirement of government is considered to have adverse effects on interest rates which in turn reduces the incentives of business to invest in productive activities (Chrystal, 1979).

III. The radical approach

One can identify three major views in radical literature on the relationship between the state and the working class and its implications for accumulation. The first view considers the state to be principally concerned with the needs of capital and the requirements of capital accumulation (Yaffe, 1973 and Hirsch, 1978). While there are different variations on this theme, some granting more and some less weight to the influence of the class struggle on state activities, the supporters of this view generally consider the capitalist state as structurally constrained by the requirements of capitalist production. Hence, the welfare state would not serve to significantly redistribute income from capital to labor. Social expenditures can only result in a form of horizontal distribution involving intra-class transfer of income. The role of social expenditures is seen in relation to the reproduction of labor power. These views are in sharp contrast with the social democratic belief in the ability of social welfare expenditures of the state to transform capitalist society bit by bit into a socialist or a post-capitalist society.

Some writers in this first group hold that some state activities may provide a counter-tendency to the falling rate of profit and economic crisis. For instance, Gamble and Walton (1976) argue that the state's intervention in the accumulation process results in the socialization of a part of the costs of constant capital which acts as a counter-tendency to the rising value composition of capital and hence may prevent the tendential fall in the rate of profit. However, they consider this a contradictory tendency, since any increase in state expenditures may have an adverse effect on the proportion of surplus value which remains available to private capital for accumulation. This should intensify the tendency of the rate of profit to fall and increase the possibility of crisis. A similar analysis is put forward by Yaffe (1973) who uses such an argument to suggest that state intervention to overcome crisis can in fact intensify the source of crisis by taxing away a part of surplus value which might have been otherwise used for accumulation and productive activity.

The second approach attributes two major functions for the state in a capitalist society. The first is to satisfy the requirements of accumulation. The second function is to keep social harmony between classes and to maintain the legitimacy of the state as well as the capitalist relations of production (O'Connor 1973). For this approach, social welfare expenditures are carried to make the capitalist social order appear as "just" and "fair" and to insure the maintenance of social harmony in society. This analysis can provide a novel interpretation of the two components of the welfare state: economic component (Keynesianism) and social component (Beveridgian aspect). Keynesianism can be viewed as a means to correct instability and make the capitalist system more productive. The task of the social or Beveridgian aspect is to guarantee social harmony and legitimation. This approach, like the previous one, maintains that welfare state expenditures would not lead to a gradual transfer of surplus value from capital to labor. However, the analysis of the legitimation function can open the door for new interpretations of the role of class struggle in shaping up the welfare state social policy. O'Connor speaks of the contradiction or trade-off between accumulation and legitimation functions of the state. In this way, the expansion of state expenditures associated with the legitimation function can have an adverse effect on accumulation. The growing struggle of workers and masses might then push the state to expand social expenditures to keep social harmony. This in turn might impair the accumulation process. Thus O'Connor's characterization of state activities provides a theoretical basis for the third trend to be explained.

The third trend identifies class struggle as a major component of the theory of the state. There is an attempt to avoid the "functionalist" approach of the above-mentioned theories by emphasizing the contradictory nature of the state and the role of the class struggle. This approach, particularly presented by Ian Gough (Gough 1979), attributes considerably more influence to the class struggle. For Gough, the formation and growth of the welfare state has been largely due to the pressure of the working class. But the effect of the class struggle in determining state policies and activities is still largely conditioned by the structure of capitalist society and the requirements of accumulation. In this way, the welfare state is not a vehicle toward socialism or a means to transfer any surplus value from capital to labor. Gough considers the development of the welfare state a contradictory one. "The welfare state", he writes, "is a product of the contradictory development of capitalist society, and in turn it has generated new contradictions which every day become more apparent" (Gough 1979: 152). He admits to the existence of a contradiction between the welfare state and capital accumulation because, "on the one hand, rising levels of state expenditures on the social services and other items are necessary to sustain the accumulation and reproduction of capital; on the other hand, the very growth of the state inhibits the accumulation of capital" (p. 105). In this way the expansion of social services are seen to retard accumulation and induce crisis. But this is not the result of the expanded net distributional gains made by working people. He rejects this possibility: "...the welfare state redistributes income within the wage-and salary-earning class (the working class, broadly conceived), not from the upper and upper-middle classes downwards, and certainly not necessarily from profits to wage incomes" (p.114). He goes even further to argue that "the return flow of welfare benefits to secure the reproduction of labor power falls far short of the taxes extracted from the working class" (p.116).

For Gough, accumulation may be retarded because state expenditures in general and "social expenses" in particular constitute an unproductive burden on the productive sector of the economy. But the degree of this influence depends on the nature of those expenditures. Following the argument of W. Semmler (1982) and J. O'Connor (1973), he asserts that although state activities are unproductive and hence a drain on surplus value, some indirectly contribute to the accumulation of capital and are therefore economically reproductive. The effect of class struggle on capital accumulation is not due to the distributional gains made by the working class through the state activities. Powerful labor movements may raise the share of wages and decrease that of profits via growing organizations at the point of production.

Another variant of this approach is presented by Samuel Bowles and Herbert Gintis for the case of the United States (Bowles-Gintis 1982), they characterize the "liberal democratic state" as an entity relatively autonomous from the accumulation of capital and its structure as being formed by social struggles. In their view, the struggle of the working class has, in fact, transformed the structure of the state and its position vis-a-vis capital and labor. The struggle of the working class for increased social expenditures has been successful in squeezing a part of the surplus value away from capital and to labor.

A major condition for accumulation of capital, in the Marxist analysis, is the separation of workers from the means of production. Bowles and Gintis argue this "dual separation" is not applicable to the conditions of liberal democratic capitalism. Hence, in advanced capitalist societies, "the impact of the state on the reserve army and the relative power of labor and capital changes decisively. The state is now a critical part of the reserve army" (Bowles and Gintis: 56). The control of capital on the supply of labor and the power of capital to extract surplus value is limited by the state. In this way the negative affect of the reserve army on wages is reduced and "this greatly interferes with the ability of capital to restore its power over labor through the normal workings of the business cycle" (p. 53). The state, then, is also able to redistribute surplus value from capital to labor through expansion of what they call citizens wages which seems to be defined by them as the distributional gains made by workers.

This version of the argument can also be found in Frances Fox Piven and Richard Cloward's analysis of the welfare state (Piven and Cloward 1985). For them, the expansion of social expenditures has adversely affected the accumulation not so much because of the transfer from capital to labor, but because "they limit profits by enlarging the bargaining power of workers with employers" (Piven and Cloward: 13). They believe the expansion of maintenance programs has weakened the function of the reserve army of labor. This has led to the rigidity of labor in recessionary periods and in this way has hampered the possibility of restructuring and revival of profit for capital.

An alternative approach is presented by Fine and Harris (1974, 1976a, and 1976b). They are critical of Gough's overpoliticisation of the theory of the state and his concentration on the sphere of exchange (distributional struggle) to explain the long-term growth of the welfare state and its commitment to full employment. For them, the fundamental resolution of crises requires the restructuring of capital to increase the rate of profit. The distributional struggle, in their view, is not of primary importance in determining the conditions of accumulation. This is because the tendential fall in the rate of profit and economic crisis are not primarily caused by rising real wages but by a rising organic composition of capital. The implication of this view is that the expansion of welfare expenditures and social wage can not be considered as the cause of the current crisis in Britain's economy and consequently the cut in the social wage or real wages can not lead to any resolution of this crisis.

IV. An evaluation

For conservatives, the competition among political parties, the pressures of interest groups, and the democratic excesses inherent in a pluralist system, overload the state with expectations which it can not satisfy. In this neoconservative logic, one would expect to observe a relative increase in social and welfare expenditures over time, particularly in the post World War II period. This is because the articulated demands of the electorate and pressure groups should be concerned more with social security and provision of social goods and services rather than expenditures on items such as infrastructure, transportation, communication and defense. In fact, conservatives place particular blame on the rise of social welfare expenditures as the major source of economic inefficiency and market distortion. But in the United Kingdom, social transfer payments and social expenditures increased rather moderately up to 1975. This moderate increase was more probably induced by such factors as urbanization, demographic changes in population, and the extension of social benefits to a larger population. It was only during the last decade that these expenditures increased disproportionately at a higher rate than other government expenditures. But here the principal cause seems to be the economic slow-down and the concomitant high levels of unemployment and inflation. This means that in contrast to the conservatives' view, the state has responded not only to the demands of the electorate but also to the perceived requirements of accumulation and the economic system. In a similar way, the argument of Bowles and Gintis, who consider class struggle as the primary source of state intervention in favor of the working class (or citizens), can not be confirmed by this empirical evidence.

On the other hand, Gough's proposition regarding the unproductive nature of state expenditures and "social expenses" and their adverse effect on accumulation is not consistent with his own conceptualization of certain state activities as reproductive. This is because within such a conceptual framework a large portion of state expenditures can be characterized as reproductive and thus helpful to capital accumulation.

In general, there is little evidence to support the existence of a causal relationship between rising state expenditures and the decline of the British economy (Hall, 1986). This is not to suggest that public sector growth has not adversely affected the economy in any form. But this must be analyzed in the broader context of the state's inability to carry on a successful economic policy and industrial strategy. As our analysis in the previous section reveals, the British state's failure to coordinate socioeconomic forces toward economic growth was directly connected with structural limits in the relationship between state, capital, and labor which was itself conditioned by particular patterns of capital accumulation in Britain and her international position.

3 Empirical studies on the distributional impact of the state budget

I. Distribution across income brackets

There are two types of studies on the redistributional activities of the state. The first group is based on a Neo-classical theoretical framework. All these studies begin with distribution of income by income brackets, and then allocate taxes and expenditures to these income brackets. The end result is the distribution of income which remains after the effects of expenditures and taxes are accounted for. This is referred to as the distribution of final or post-redistribution incomes. In the United Kingdom, major studies of this type are Carter (1955), Nicholson (1962, 1964, 1968, 1970, 1972), and Stephenson (1976). There are several critiques to be made of these studies. First, the studies take the income of families as the base to calculate taxes paid and benefits received by them. Not only income but size of the family, age of the members, number of dependents and the like have an effect on taxes and benefits. Second, these studies do not take into account intergenerational redistribution affected by social expenditures, especially social security. The influences of pension funds is to transfer income from the employed to the retired. If age was considered, the pension payment might involve no distribution (Alkinson and Stiglitz, 1980: Chap.9). Third, these studies in fact involve a comparison of the general equilibrium of the economy with and without the government budget. From our point of view, this is meaningless because there is no instance in society in which government does not exist. Although such studies contain much useful information, their basic framework is entirely inadequate for our purposes of studying income differences caused by class differences. The tax incidence assumptions of these studies are rooted in such a theoretical approach.

Finally, the distribution across the income brackets approach is consistent with the view of the state acting from without to improve the shortcomings of "Pareto optimality" or imperfections in the market to satisfy the principles of justice and equity and not as a response to class pressure or the requirement of capital accumulation. All income groups are then treated qualitatively as equal since all receive their income under the same conditions, selling factors of production they own and receiving what they are worth; the criterion is their marginal contribution to production. The difference in income is conceived as the outcome of the difference in marginal productivity of factors (things) and not membership in different social classes.

Moreover, these studies are usually carefully conducted within their own conceptual framework, providing some valuable information on income groups and sometimes useful methods of measurement to be considered. But they do not provide us with any direct information on distributional gains of the working class or capital and consequently do not measure the influence of social services on capital accumulation and economic growth. The findings of these studies contain useful information regarding "vertical redistribution" which can be used as an indirect means to analyze the benefit/burden position of the working population with respect to state expenditures and taxes. It is thus useful to review the methodology and results of a few of these studies. It will be shown that these results are in general consistent with the findings of our own study. The studies selected for review are Nicholson (1966), Nicholson (1972), and Stephenson (1976).

1. Methodology and assumptions

The underlying assumptions of these works are very similar. It is, therefore, more appropriate to explain the assumptions of all these three studies at the same time. These studies first divide the households into several groups with different ranges of original income, and then allocate the incidence of taxes and benefits to these ranges. The original income is defined as income before any taxes and benefits. This is a more practical starting point and is not completely consistent with the no-government position in Neo-classical theory. This is because money incomes before taxes and benefits cannot be equated with incomes as they would be in the hypothetical absence of any state activity.

There are two groups of taxes: direct and indirect taxes. Direct taxes on personal income include income tax and surtax and employees' contributions to National Insurance and National Health Services. The allocation of these taxes to households in different categories of income does not involve any particular difficulty. Death duties and taxes on capital gains are excluded on the basis that both are a tax on capital rather than income. The omission of the second type is problematic, since capital gains can be included in personal income in which case capital gains tax should be regarded as a direct tax on income.

More difficulties arise when we deal with indirect taxes or taxes on expenditure of the household sector. These taxes are either paid directly by consumers, such as local rates and motor vehicle duties, or are assumed to be fully reflected in prices paid by consumers when buying those goods which are subject to purchase tax, or customs, or excise duties. It is thus assumed that retail prices fully reflect indirect expenditure taxation. This assumption is based on the Neo-classical theory of tax incidence in which the introduction of any tax of this type leads to a change in prices of the related goods, the degree of which depends on elasticity's of demand and supply. This approach differs from the one developed in Classical and Marxian political economy in which indirect taxes are assumed to be primarily borne by profit (or surplus value). In the book, the second type of assumption with respect to indirect expenditure taxes is used.

Employers' contributions to National Insurance have been regarded as part of employees' income and as a tax on these incomes in the studies done prior to 1969. The studies conducted from this date, i.e., Nicholson (1972) and Stephenson (1976), have treated these contributions as an indirect tax. This is based on a theoretical argument that employers' contributions form an integral part of labor costs and as such contribute to changes in prices.

Benefits are divided into two groups. The first group includes those benefits paid directly to the household in the form of cash or benefits in kind. Cash benefits are National Insurance benefits (excluding scholarships and education grants), Pensions, and Family Allocations. Benefits in kind include the National Health Services, State Education (including scholarships and education grants), school health services, school meals, milk and welfare foods. To measure the share of households in educational expenses, it is assumed that all children at all types of educational establishments derive the same benefit. This assumption is problematic because it does not take into account segregation in schooling and the differentiation in the quality and facilities of education in different localities whose residents may vary in term of wealth, income, or racial and ethnic background. Thus the assumption made in this dissertation that families benefit from state education in proportion to their income levels is preferable (see the following Chapter).

For National Health Services, it is assumed that the value of their services is identical for all persons in each of six age and sex categories of the population, and is equal to the estimated average expenditure by the state per person. Further, it is assumed that the value of health services received by the working population is proportional to the share of their earnings in personal income.[1]

Some other items, such as administration, defense, police, and prisons are not counted as the benefit of households. Nicholson (1972) considers defense, police and prisons to be "regrettable necessities" rather than benefits to families. The administration of National Insurance and Supplementary Benefits, and the upkeep of local offices are considered to be the necessary costs of providing social services but not yet benefits to families.

Other items, of public goods and services, such as roads and public lighting, water, sewerage and refuse disposal, public health services, parks and pleasure grounds, libraries, museums and the arts, fire service, and welfare services, are not allocated as benefits received by families due to the difficulty involved in the measurement of their value for any individual family. But it is argued that this omission should not lead to any significant distortion of results, since they constitute a relatively small portion of government expenditures. The only indirect benefits counted in these studies are housing subsidies the value of which are estimated as the excess of the estimated economic rent (or market-determined rent) over what the tenants of local authority dwellings actually pass as rent. Agricultural subsidies are not included as any benefit received by farmers, since their purpose is to increase the earnings of farmers to the level of average income of workers in other types of employment. The main objective of these subsidies is not to assist poor farmers to augment their standard of living, but to keep domestic prices as low as the prices of imported food.

2. The findings of these studies

If we look at the relative significance of taxation's alone, we can conclude that direct and indirect taxes combined form a stable proportion of income over a wide range of incomes but they absorb a smaller fraction of the income of the very rich than of the very poor. This has been the case for all the years for which these studies are conducted. In 1971 taxes absorbed on average about 38 percent of original income or 35 percent of gross income (original income plus cash benefits from the state). In 1976 in the case of households comprising two adults and one to four children taxes absorbed about 36 per cent from the original incomes of the top decile, and slightly more from the other families but for the poorest tenth total tax payments took away about 44 per cent of their original incomes.

The bite of other kinds of taxation on the very poor was even more harsh. For example, a non-retired family of two adults in the lowest decile range of income paid around 63 per cent of their income in taxes, while this ratio was about 40 per cent for other families of the same size from the rich down to the near poor (see Westergaard 1978: 76). Hence, the conclusion is that taxation has not positively reshaped inequalities; if anything it has widened the inequality between the rich and the poor.

While taxation had a regressive outcome, the distribution of benefits among families in different ranges of income have been sufficiently progressive to outweigh the net regressive effect of taxes. Here, the term progressive in the case of benefits means that it forms a larger proportion of low than high incomes. .

This conclusion can be confirmed by both studies by Nicholson for 1971 and Stephenson for 1976. The general results of the first study is set out in Table 3.1. It shows that families in the lowest income ranges receive more in benefits than they pay in taxes, while families in the highest deciles pay rather more in taxes than they receive in benefits. For families of all types the break-even point is reached at the income range of £987 to £1193. Families belonging to this income range pay almost the same amount in taxes as they gain in benefits. Families below this level of income receive some net gain from the redistribution activities of the state, while families with an income above this level have to pay a net tax. But the net benefit or the net tax for the middle income households is not substantial.

Table 3.1
Net benefit/tax position of households, 1971
(all figures in pounds per year)

	range of original income: pounds per year												average 3750 and over	overall income ranges
Under 381	381	461	557	674	816	987	1194	1446	1749	2116	2562	3099		
All households in the same														
494	39	303	250	193	62	-5	-136	-242	-359	-472	-672	-885	-1594	-259
Retired households														
1 adult														
358	174	115	39	24	-46	-136		-293						+273
2 adults														
546	373	329	288	150	218	45	42	-251	-411					+383
Non-retired households														
1 adult														
339	115	15	-20	-91	-250	-286	-393	-590	-713	-836		-1428		-250
2 adults														
511	465	254	367	204	-18	-139								
2 adults, 1 child														
992			224	45	-122	-216	-310	-486	-546	-754	-914	-1505		-423
2 adults, 2 children														
840		203	99	78	-66	-186	-288	-409	-591	-808	-1312			-3282
2 adults, 3 children														
			456	213	141	-65	-95	-260	-264	-512	-1227			-1003
2 adults, 4 children														
			453	365	164	124	129	-154						41

Source: Nicholson (1972: 76)

Thus the conclusion that can be drawn from this study is that there is some redistribution of income from the richest households to the poorest households. However, we have to pay attention to the fact that the net tax paid by higher income households is not entirely used to finance welfare and public assistance and other benefits received by the poor. It is also used to finance some general expenditures of the state, such as defense, police, judiciary system, administration and some other public goods, such as highways, parks, libraries, museums, etc. which are not included in the Nicholson's study (and other studies of this type).

The estimates of this study are confined to showing the average effects on "vertical inequality" between income ranges for the six types of family combined, but do not directly address the question of "horizontal redistribution" between different sizes and types of family. However, it is possible to estimate the progressiveness or regressiveness of taxes and benefits for any particular size and type of family in different income ranges. In general, for a given income range the families of larger size gain most (or lose least) and the families of smaller size gain least (or lose most) from the impact of all taxes and benefits combined. The smaller the income of the family and the larger the size of the family, the greater is the net gain (or the smaller is the net loss), while the families of larger income and smaller size are bound to have a larger net loss (or a smaller net gain) from taxes and benefits as a proportion of income.

Thus non-retired families consisting of one adult paid more in taxes than they received in benefits if they had an initial income of more than approximately £550. On the other hand, retired households with one adult could have received an income of between £557 and £674 per annum without reaching the point at which they paid more in taxes than they received in benefits. A family of two adults and two children could have received up to £987 before reaching this 'break even' point. The break even point for a family of two adults and four children was substantially higher, between £2116 and £2561.

The results of Stephenson's study for 1976 are summarized in Table 3.2. Within each household type, households are ranked in deciles according to their original incomes. The highest decile includes the initially richest ten percent of the total number of households. The lowest decile consists of the initially poorest ten percent among all households. 'Final' income is defined as income after deduction of all allocated taxes (direct and indirect) and after taking into account all state benefits in cash and allocated state benefits in kind at their estimated money value. The figures shown in this Table are average final incomes expressed as a percentage of average original incomes. Figures above 100 indicate net gain, i.e., benefit values exceeded tax payments, while figures below 100 indicate a net loss for families involved after the effects of taxes and benefits are counted.

Table 3.2
The net impact of state benefits and taxation on the income of households, 1976
(average final income expressed as a percentage of average original income)

Decline of original income within each household type	Households of following type, comprising:					
	Non-retired		2 adults and	Other	Retired	
	1 adult	2 adults	1-4 children	retired	1 adult	2 adults
Highest decile	56	62	75	70	107	86
9th decile	62	64	79	73	154	138
8th decile	60	65	81	75	231	186
7th decile	67	65	83	77	329	245
6th decile	67	68	86	81	469	336
5th decile	72	70	87	89	492	437
4th decile	89	77	92	101		572
3rd decile	120	86	97	116	7788	
2nd decile	195	107	103	161		2476
lowest decile	1086	252	188	789		
All households of stated type	75	73	87	88	303	221
Percentage of all households accounted for by each type	9	23	26	21	12	9

Source: Wetergaard (1978: 79)

The results clearly indicate that there was a transfer of resources within each income hierarchy, from higher income families to those whose income was initially low. The Table also shows that the pattern has been consistently progressive. When there were net gains, they were proportionally higher for the initially poorer households; where there were net losses, they increased with the increase of the original incomes of the households in question.

The households who have received net gains of substance as a result of a vertical redistribution of income are the poorest households (the lowest two deciles for non-retired households). Other non-retired households have ended up paying more in taxes than they have received in benefits. This means that the majority of working class families did not receive any net benefit from the welfare state intervention in this year. This pattern is consistent with the results of our study. As we will see in Chapter five, the net "social wage" received by the working population would be insignificant or negative during the late 1970's and 1980's if we did not include Public Assistance and Welfare which is largely received by the poor.

It is clear from the Table that the only groups of non-retired households who receive any positive net benefit from the state are the lowest income groups. In relative terms, the net gain by the lowest decile seems to be substantial. But the absolute value of the net benefits received by a poor family is not necessarily substantial. Just because the poor start with little original income, the relative value of the benefits they obtain is very high when measured as a percentage of their original income. Our own study shows (see Chapter four) that, in fact, the cost of financing Public Assistance and Welfare has significantly increased over the last decade. But this is not due to an increase in the amount of benefits received by each poor family. The increased cost is the result of the persistent high unemployment rate and the increased proportion of low paying jobs.

An important conclusion that we can derive from this study is that much of the positive redistribution which does occur in the end is "horizontal". This conclusion can be clearly drawn by looking at the net gains (or net loss) of "all households of stated type" in Table 3.2. The households who have received substantial net benefits are the retired households whose original incomes are usually substantially lower than other households. Other non-retired families have on the average paid more in taxes than they have received in benefits. The redistribution primarily involves transfers between people at different stages of life. The Table shows transfers from childless adults of working age and to a lesser extent from families with children to elderly people who have reached retirement. But none of this "horizontal" redistribution on its own alters the overall inequality between classes. The welfare system involves a massive intra-class redistribution, from the adults of working age to the retired and from the employed to the unemployed and the incapacitated. As Westergaard (1978:81) has stated, "state provision of 'age directed' beneficial has modified the character of the 'proletarian condition', because it has helped to reduce those fluctuations of life cycle experience which have traditionally exposed people of the wage earning class to special risk of poverty in childhood, parenthood and old age (as also in unemployment and in sickness)".

Table 3.3 presents the Gini Coefficient for income distribution before and after the allocation of state benefits and taxes. The Gini Coefficients are expressed in percentage form and can vary between extreme limits of 0 (when all incomes are equal) and 100 (when all income goes to only one individual). Thus the larger the coefficient, the greater is the degree of inequality, and a given reduction in the value of the coefficient measures the extent to which inequality has been reduced.

Table 3.3
Gini coefficients of vertical inequality

	1961-2	1962-3	1963-4	1964-5	1965-6	1967	1968	1969	1970	1971
Weighted average of Gini coefficient for six main types of families										
1. Original income	31.3	32.4	32.9	31.3	30.6	31.2	32.1	33.3	33.4	34.0
2. Income after direct benefits	25.2	26.0	26.5	24.8	23.8	24.3	24.5	25.4	25.7	25.9
3. Income after direct taxes and benefits	23.0	23.5	24.1	22.7	21.6	22.0	22.4	22.7	22.9	23.4
4. Income after all taxes and benefits	24.3	24.9	25.9	24.7	23.5	23.8	24.7	24.8	24.7	25.0
Percentage reduction in Gini coefficient from										
5. Direct benefits	19.4	19.8	19.6	21.0	22.0	22.2	23.8	23.7	23.1	23.8
6. Direct taxes and benefits	26.6	27.6	26.8	27.5	29.2	29.7	30.1	31.8	31.5	31.2
7. All taxes and benefits	22.3	23.2	21.4	21.3	23.1	23.6	22.8	25.4	26.1	26.4

Source: Nicholson (1972: 79)

What is interesting is that the distribution of income has changed so little over a period of ten years. Changes in economic and social structure which might have large effects on particular groups have had little influence on the overall form of income distribution (Nicholson 1972: 78). While the inequality in original income has slightly increased, the degree of inequality of final income throughout this period has remained the same. In 1961-2 the Gini Coefficient for pre-redistribution incomes was 31.5 and for post-redistribution incomes was 22.3. In 1971, the comparable coefficients were 34.0 and 26.4. This means that the rise in inequality of original income has been largely offset by an increase in the extent of redistribution through all taxes and benefits. The combined effect of all taxes and benefits was to reduce inequality by close to 23 percent in 1960, and by about 26 percent in 1971.

The stability of the vertical inequality over time will appear to be even more remarkable when Barna's estimate of 1937 is compared with Nicholson's estimate for this period. Nicholson has adjusted the Gini-Coefficients obtained by Barna to take into account the differences in method. The coefficients arrived of in this way would have been 33 for the level of inequality of the original income and 25 for that of final income which are more or less the same as those of the more recent years (see Table 3.3). This shows that the post-war developments of the welfare state have had little effect on vertical redistribution.

In short, the findings of these studies show that the welfare state has not significantly contributed to a growth of equality in the United Kingdom. The primary impact of the "welfare state" is to reduce horizontal inequality among different sections of the working population. Coupled with extensive "horizontal" redistribution, there is also some limited vertical redistribution directed towards the lowest income groups comprising of the poor families whose adult members are either detached from the labor force or working at very low pay jobs. Most of the wage earning households, except those on very low incomes, contribute significantly to the "welfare state" to finance other expenditures such as defense, police, judiciary, and the provision of certain public goods and services which are not taken into account in the above studies. The welfare state has done little to alter the aggregate inequality between classes. In large measures, "the role of the welfare state has been in guaranteeing a minimum income against the natural calamities of life-sickness, unemployment, and some protection against ill health" (Wedderburn 1965: 135). This is the conclusion which is, in general, in line with the findings of our research to be presented in the following Chapter.

II. The distributional impact on classes: A general review of major studies

The second set of studies include Bowles and Gintis (1982), Anwar Shaikh[2] (1978) for the U.S. and Ian Gough (1979) in the U.K.

The first one by Bowles and Gintis covers several years in the Post-War period of the U.S. Their results imply the existence of a positive and considerable "citizen wage" (or net distributional gains made by working people). As an example, their data for 1965 give a "citizen wage of 22 percent and for 1977, of 59 percent of the gross earnings of an average production and non-supervisory worker. Therefore, the "citizen wage" is considered to be very large relative to the total wage as well as growing through time.

They reject the idea of the "wages-push" profit squeeze. They correctly remind us that the "increase in the share of employee compensation in national income does not indicate a wage squeeze but rather the shift of the labor force out of self-employment into paid employment" (p. 70). We may add to this argument that this increase is at least partly due to the relative expansion of unproductive activities including state expenditures. Their additional argument that "the bookkeeping convention that counts the employer's payroll taxes toward social insurance as employee compensation rather than as before-tax profit" is responsible for this increase, seems doubtful. They should first establish that employers' payroll tax is not actually part of the wage fund.

While they reject the "wage squeeze" interpretations of the current crisis, they support, what we may call, a citizen wage-squeeze analysis of the current crisis. "The major distributional gains made by workers (in their view) were not achieved in their direct confrontation with capital over the bargaining table, but in the state. The working class has increasingly relied upon the citizen wage as the concrete form of its distributional victories"(p. 70).

In their view, the major force behind the current crisis is "a fall in the rate of profit through a decline in the rate of relative surplus value". This decline in the rate of relative surplus value is, in turn, mainly induced by "a gradual redistribution of the total product away from capital and a decreased ability of the reserve army to discipline labor" (pp.84, 85) and intensified by some other transformations like the deterioration in the terms of trade and rising input prices. To establish their analysis empirically, they present two sets of data: one indicating a decline in both before and after tax rates of return on capital and another set implying increase in the distributional gains of the workers or what they call "citizen wage."

As we mentioned before, the decline in the rate of profit during the past decades is admitted by several other studies. The question, though, is the factor explaining this decline. Further to the "wage squeeze" theory noted before, there is a Marxian argument developed by Marx himself and supported by several Marxists. The latter analysis bases itself on the argument of tendential increases in organic composition of capital (Shaikh 1978a,1978b). To prove their point, Bowles and Gintis need not only establish the decline in the profit rate but also to show this decline is not due to other causes explained by other theories. They need either to show other theories go wrong theoretically and/or can not be supported by the empirical evidence or at least to establish the existence of a strong increase in the distributional gains made by the working class. The latter is the path they choose to proceed. Thus, they not only provide a theoretical analysis to make their view established, but also conduct an empirical study based on the U.S. data for several years in the Post-War II period to show a transfer of surplus value away from capital and to working people has been the reality. And this is exactly what this book is about. It is the objective of this study to test this hypothesis for the last decades in the United Kingdom.

The other empirical study on this subject for the U.S. is the pioneer work by Shaikh in "National Accounts and Marxian Categories" (1978).[3] Shaikh's calculation covers three years and he finds out that taxes paid by workers in recent decades have been even *greater* than benefits received by them in the form of social welfare expenditures. His calculation yields a net tax (negative social wage) of $15,060 million for 1952, $12,077 million for 1961 and $24,695 million for 1970.

Ian Gough's (1979) work on the United Kingdom does not directly measure the transfer between state and workers. His own calculations cover only certain aspects of the subject matter; and he generally uses and interprets the data available for social expenditures, taxes and the distributional implication of the state budget on income brackets. His conclusion is that "the return flow of welfare benefits to secure the reproduction of labor power falls far short of the taxes extracted from the working class" (p. 116) excluding that portion of social services consumed by the non-working population. He concludes that there is no necessity "to assume that the growth of welfare state will inevitably reduce the quantity of surplus value in the capitalist sector and thus inhibit accumulation and growth." (p. 117)

He argues that whereas the struggle of the working class was a determining factor in achieving a more developed social security system, other factors like rising costs, changing population structures and the emergence of new needs would probably account for almost all of the growth in expenditures since World War II. Lower productivity growth in the public sector (social services being labor intensive) accompanied by growing unionization and militancy of public workers imply a relative increase in the costs of social services. The rise in the proportion of elderly in the total population and this greater separation from their immediate families requires more social expenditures by the state. On the other hand, the development of capitalism generates new needs to be satisfied. The expansion of welfare expenditures may not be even sufficient to satisfy the growing needs. In general, very little or no improvement is seen by him in the satisfaction of needs.

Gough's own study does not, however, provide systematic empirical evidence for the net benefit/burden of the working class in the U.K. to support his assertion about the effect of the welfare state on the accumulation of capital. His main definition for the social wage is the "flow of welfare benefits in cash and in kind back to the employed and non-employed population"(p. 108). He includes both transfer payments, such as social security, unemployment insurance, etc., and socialized consumption like health, education, housing and community development etc. There are two problems with this particular concept of the social wage. First, this definition of the social wage concentrates on the expenditure side of the government activities and disregards the taxation side. In other words, this is a gross concept of the social wage which is not net of taxes paid by workers. In contrast, the concept of the "citizen wage" in Bowles-Gintis and of "net tax" in Shaikh from the start account for both benefits received and taxes paid by workers. The second problem rests with Gough's description of recipients of the benefits for in his conceptualization of the social wage, the employed and non-employed are included. This concept (of non-employed) in his definition is too broad and too vague.

For empirical evidence, he presents the measurement of flows between the "personal" and the state sector for the U.K. in 1975 (Gough 1979, p. 109). The results of his estimation are summarized in Table 3.4.

Table 3.4
Flows between the personal and state sectors, 1975

£ billion	Personal sector	State sector
Income from employment	60.0	
Income from self-employment	8.7	
Income from property	2.1	
Total personal income	70.8	
Income tax	-15.6	+15.6
National insurance contributions	-2.8	+2.8
Social-security benefits and other transfers	+9.4	-9.4
Disposable incomes	61.8	
Net savings	-0.3	
Consumption expenditure	61.6	
Indirect taxes	-10.8	+10.8
Subsidies	+3.2	-3.2
Real consumption	54.0	
Social services in kind	+11.4	-11.4
Private and 'social' consumption	65.4	
Net transfers	-5.2	+5.2

This is a reproduction of Table 4.1 in Gough, 1979: 109.

Gough's personal sector consists of households who receive benefits from the state and in return pay taxes to the state. The income of the households comes from labor, property and state benefits. His schema can not account for any figure for a proper concept of the social wage, because the personal sector includes not only the workers but also the self-employed and even capitalist families. He himself concludes that his estimation "shows the importance of the social wage in the United Kingdom... ignoring subsidies, the social services in cash and in kind amounted to almost 21 billion pounds in 1975, approaching 30 percent of personal incomes" (p. 110). The net transfer resulting from the state's distributive activities in 1975 was a flow of 5.2 billion pounds from the personal sector to the state.

This estimation of the social wage is quite problematic. It does not make any distinction between social classes or between working and non-working segments of the working class. While he is aware of this fact, he does not provide us with a more careful estimation of the social wage. He admits that his estimation "does not discriminate between households which receive their income from labor, from those whose income stems from property or from the state benefits themselves" (p. 108). Therefore his own estimation of the net flow from the personal sector to the state sector can not provide an objective basis for the conclusion he would like to provide that "the return flow of welfare benefits to secure the reproduction of labor power falls far short of the taxes extracted from working class" (p. 116). In fact, the resulting positive and significant net transfer from the household sector to the state sector is something that should have been expected.

On the tax side, he takes into account both direct income taxes and indirect expenditure taxes in their entirety as a burden for households. On the expenditure side, he counts those expenditures which have any direct influence on the standards of living of households. These include both the benefits received from social services (i.e., Social Insurance, Public Assistance and Welfare, Education and Health) and the value of the return from "collective consumption" (which includes public goods and services consumed by households). It is not quite clear from his analysis which categories of public goods and services have been included in his estimation of the "collective consumption" of the household sector. But it is clear that his estimation does not include these items of state expenditures, such as military, police, judiciary, infrastructure, and subsidies to the private sector. Thus the conclusion that we can actually derive from his empirical exercise is that not only social services and items of collective consumption, but also the bulk of the latter categories of state expenditures are financed by the direct and indirect taxes paid by households and this should have been self-evident.

The methodology adopted in this book for the estimation of the "net social wage" in the United Kingdom has been based on the comparative analysis of Shaikh (1978) and Bowles and Gintis (1982). Hence a review of the concepts and methods used in these two studies will be very useful. In the following, we will review the general methodology of these two studies, and then compare their conceptual frameworks and the methods applied to estimate the share of the working population in the categories of state expenditures and taxes.

1. The general methodological approach

Bowles and Gintis first estimate the citizen wage for a family of four with one employed as a production and non-supervisory worker, for several years in the post-war period. The results, as we mentioned before, imply a positive and significant "citizen wage" (see Bowles and Gintis, 1982, Table 3). These results are presented in Table 3.5. The first four columns are the exact reproduction of

Table 3 in their study. We have added two columns to their Table (columns 5 and 6) to present the estimation of the net social wage (or "citizen wage" as they call it) and the net social wage ratio. Net social wage is the difference between estimated weekly social welfare expenditures and estimated weekly direct taxes on earning (columns 4 and 2). On the last columns, the net social wage ratio is the ratio of net social wage over gross average weekly earning. On the basis of their results, the working population has substantially benefited from the redistributive activities of the state. A typical working class family (a production and non-supervisory worker with three dependents in their study) has received far more in benefits than what they have paid in taxes. The net gain of such a family has been significant in all years of their study and has also grown substantially over years. Their study indicates that weekly real net benefits received by a typical family have increased from 13 dollars in 1948 to 61 dollars in 1977. This means that the net social wage has increased by close to 500 percent over the period of their study, from 1948 to 1977. Their results also imply that the net social wage has considerably contributed to the standards of living of the working population. The net social wage ratio or the share of the average weekly net gain of this typical working class family in its gross average weekly earnings has risen from 15 percent in 1948 to 57 percent in 1977. This is a surprisingly high ratio. This trend implies a substantial decline in the working class dependency on the labor market in order to earn their subsistence. Such a trend represents a considerable transformation in the role of the state and the capitalist structure of production in the United States.

Table 3.5
Sources of workers' consumption:
The wage and the citizen wage, 1948-1977, in constant (1967) dollars

Year	Gross Average Weekly Earnings[a] (1)	Est. Weekly Direct Taxes on Earnings[b] (2)	Spendable Average Weekly Earnings[c] (3)	Est. Weekly Social Welfare Expenditures[d] (4)	Net Social Wage or Citizen Wage (5)	Net Social Wage Ratio (6)
1948	68	1	67	14	13	0.19
1950	74	2	72	16	14	0.18
1955	84	5	79	19	14	0.16
1959	96	9	82	25	16	0.16
1965	101	10	91	32	22	0.21
1972	109	12	97	61	47	0.43
1977	104	10	94	71		0.59

Average Annual Rate of Growth, 1948-1977
    1.5%   7.9%   1.2%   5.6%

Increase, 1948-1977
    36   9   26   5

Note: a. Gross average weekly earnings of production and non-supervisory workers, in 1967 dollars.
b. Estimated weekly direct taxation (including employee contributions to social insurance) for production or non-supervisory workers, in 1967 dollars.
c. Spend able average weekly earnings of production or non-supervisory workers, in 1967 dollars, for a worker with three dependents.
d. Estimated weekly social welfare expenditures under public programs per family of four, in 1967 dollars.

Source: Table 3 in Bowles and Gintis (1982).

But this in itself, even if we assume their method of measurement is correct, does not present any evidence for the existence of an overall positive citizen wage. They, in fact, should have implicitly assumed that the size of an average production worker family is four. Otherwise, the result they would like to derive will not be meaningful. Anwar Shaikh (in his unpublished notes on the "Social Wage") has clearly shown that the size of an average family cannot be four and the number of employed members is certainly more than one. He divides the population by the number of households to get the average number of people per household. This figure comes to 3.14 for 1970. He further divides the number of employed by the number of households and gets 1.24 workers per household (for 1970). He then estimates the "citizen wage" using Bowles and Gintis' method and it comes to be quite smaller. Using his own method, (for an average family) he finds that the "citizen wage" is not a significant figure.

If we refine somewhat Shaikh's estimation of the number of workers per household, the figure comes to be even bigger. In fact not all households have members in the labor force, some families are totally separated from the labor force and, hence, cannot be considered as part of the working class population (the "dead weight" of the reserve army in Marx). Furthermore, a number of these families are those of the self-employed. Now if we divide the number of employed (excluding the self-employed) by the number of families whose source of income is wages and salary, we get approximately two employed workers per family for 1979. (See Statistical Abstract of the U.S. 1981, Tables 659 and 740).

The size of a working class family, however, has to be slightly smaller than Shaikh's estimation. Those families having no member in the labor force are generally of a relatively large size on the average. In 1969 the average size of a family below the poverty level was close to five (calculation based on data from the same source, Table 552). Many of these families are separated from the labor force (but not all). If we adjust our figure, the average size of a worker's family will be slightly smaller than Shaikh's estimation. Actual "citizen wage" has to be even smaller than Shaikh's estimations (in his Notes...) and using his method we will probably get negative figures for the net social wage.

There is another inconsistency in Bowles and Gintis' measurement. While they include the expenditures of the government both at the federal and state and local level, they do not include taxes paid by the average production worker to the state and local governments (Shaikh: Notes...).

In contrast to Bowles and Gintis, Shaikh's methodology in "National Income Account... " is to estimate the aggregate taxes paid by all wage-earners and total benefits received by them from state expenditures. This method seems to give a more accurate estimation procedure. Bowles and Gintis' average production worker receiving an average earning and having a number of dependents is not to be necessarily the representative of all production workers and even less that of all workers. There are those younger production workers having fewer dependents but lower salaries belonging to a lower tax bracket but claiming fewer exemptions. There are older production workers having probably more dependents but receiving a higher salary. We may consider the retired who receive more transfer payments (pension and Medicare) and paying few taxes. There is no reason to assume that the family of this production worker is an average representative of all families of the working population in terms of taxes paid and benefits received. For all the workers, the matter becomes even more difficult. There are those blue collar non-production workers who earn lower income and hence may pay lower taxes and receive more benefits. On the other hand, a relatively large number of illegal immigrant workers pay taxes without receiving transfer payments. There are white collar non-production workers with similar salary or above. If we were able actually to find a representative working-class family, this model would give a more exact estimation of taxes. But this is exactly the difficulty. The aggregate approach does not run into these difficulties.

The second step in Bowles and Gintis' measurement is the calculation of total workers' consumption, including both their consumption financed from returns to labor and social welfare expenditures. Their results (Table 5 in Bowles and Gintis, 1982) indicate a minor increase (only in the 1970's) in total workers' consumption as a fraction of total output, while consumption financed from returns to labor has relatively declined as a percentage of total output. This has happened due to the increase in social welfare expenditures both as a fraction of GNP and as that of total workers' consumption. Then they measure the net share of capital in total output for which their results (Table 6 in Bowles and Gintis, 1982) indicate a significant decline in recent decades. Their results are included in Table 3.6. As this Table shows, total workers' consumption's as a fraction of the total output has increased from 66 percent in 1948 to 70 percent in 1977. For the same period, the net share of capital in total output has declined from 16 percent to 7 percent.

Table 3.6
The percentage share of workers' consumption and capital in total output

	1948	1950	1955	1959	1965	1972	1977
I Consumption Financed Returns							
(1)	.58	.58	.55	.55	.54	.52	.51
Social Welfare Expenditures							
(2)	.08	.08	.08	.10	.11	.19	.19
Total Workers' Consumption							
(3)	.66	.66	.63	.65	.65	.71	.70
Social Welfare as a Fraction of Total Consumption							
(4)	.12	.13	.13	.15	.17	.27	.27
II Capital's Gross Share							
(5)	.34	.34	.37	.35	.35	.29	.30
Reproduction of Constant Capital							
(6)	.07	.07	.09	.09	.08	.10	.10
Government Costs Not Related to Expenditures							
(7)	.11	.12	.15	.15	.15	.14	.13
Capital's Net Share							
(8)	.16	.14	.13	.09	.12	.05	.07

Source: Table 5 and 6 in Bowles and Gintis (1982)

Their conclusion is "that part of the total product consumed by wage-and-salary workers, expressed as a fraction of gross national product, has gradually but significantly increased. All of the increase may be attributed to the growth of social wage expenditures from 8 to 19 percent of the total output. The claim of property-income recipients on total output has correspondingly declined" (p.75).

The Table does not imply any gradual but significant increase in total consumption of workers as a fraction of GNP. This ratio has even slightly declined in the decades prior to 1965. The only significant increase in this ratio is from 1965 to 1972 from 65 percent to 71 percent. What their results imply is, more than anything else, the growing significance of public goods and transfer payments in workers' satisfaction of their needs and a relative decline in the share of marketed commodities in the consumption of workers. While this may have a secondary implication for the accumulation of capital it has nothing to do with the increasing value of net "citizen wage". In our previous remarks, we explained the part of problem with their calculation of "citizen wage". Now we find out that, in fact, their own results in Table 5 are not consistent with the significant increase in "citizen wage".

In the measurement of social expenditures, they include Public Assistance and Veterans' benefits. The first item is comprised of the benefits in cash and in kind received by the poor. The main part of these benefits is not received by the labor force. The inclusion of this item as an integral part of the social wage requires some qualifications which will be discussed in the following Chapter. Veterans' benefits, as Shaikh (1978) has argued, is a cost of war. The recipients of these benefits are mostly the working population households. But they receive these benefits not as workers but as soldiers of past wars. These two items are partially responsible for the increase in total workers' consumption from 1965 to 1972. Veterans benefits almost doubled and public assistance and welfare increased by more than three times. The other major factor is a substantial increase in taxes in this period. Table 3 of their study shows that in this period, total wages as a percentage of domestic income of the non-financial sector increased by 3 percent (from 66 percent in 1965 to 69 percent in 1972), while consumption financed by returns to labor as a fraction of GNP, declined by 2 percent. This means that workers paid proportionally a higher level of taxes and in return received benefits from the state. In fact both taxes paid by workers and benefits received by them increased substantially in this period. This fact, as we saw, can be derived from their own study when we compare tables 2 and 3. Other studies (Tonak 1984, Fazeli-Fazeli 1984) show that workers both in 1965 and 1972 paid more taxes what they received in benefits. Therefore even in this period (and especially in this period), workers' consumption of public goods and the consumption of marketed goods financed by transfer payments increased relative to their consumption of marketed commodities. Any improvement in their material conditions was due to an increase in real wages (see Table 3 in Bowles and Gintis, 1982) and not in "citizen wage". The declining share of capital in total output then has to be explained by factors other than the growing "citizen wage".

2. *The conceptual differences in the two studies*

We have already mentioned that Bowles and Gintis include only direct taxes paid by workers to the federal government, neglecting taxes paid to state and local governments. The other difference on the tax side is on the inclusion of employers' contribution for social security. In their argument against the "wage squeeze" approach,

Bowles and Gintis assert that the inclusion of this item as part of employees' compensation (in the official data) is simply a bookkeeping convention and treat that as a transfer from before-tax profits. Following this logic, they opt not to include this item in taxes paid by workers; but Anwar Shaikh does. Counting this item as employee compensation is more than a bookkeeping convention.

Employers' contributions are not a tax on profits which will increase or decline when the amount of profit increases or declines. To hire workers, capital has to pay not only direct wages but also employers' contributions the size of which will depend (in some ranges of wages) on the wages and salaries of employees not on profit. For the business firm any decision to hire additional workers will depend not only on direct wages but also employers' contributions. It is clear that this will constitute a cost of labor for capital the size of which will affect direct wages. This is a wage cost which has to be considered as a part of variable capital rather than surplus value (or profit) or constant capital. Hence, this has to be considered as a tax paid by labor and not capital. Nicholson (1972) has also counted this item as an integral part of wages.

On the expenditure side, Bowles and Gintis include veterans benefits and public assistance as part of benefits received by workers. Both items are not counted as workers' benefits by Anwar Shaikh.

Veterans benefits are considered as the "cost of war" by Shaikh and consequently not any part of workers' gains in general. This is a more appropriate treatment of this category. While many of those who receive this benefit are members of the working people, they receive it, however, not as workers but as soldiers who have participated in past wars. This is not a payment to serve the reproduction of the working people as workers but is a necessary cost for the reproduction of the system the same as military expenditures.

Public assistance is not counted by Shaikh on the grounds that it is not received by the working population but by those who are separated from the labor force. This, in fact, is payment to the poor who constitute the "dead weight" (in Marx's words) of the industrial reserve army. This is not part of workers' income but "it enters into the faux frais (incidental expenses) of capitalist production."

In O'Connor's view (O'Connor 1975), as well as in Gough's account, this is part of "social expenses" which serves the legitimating of capital and hence does not enter into the costs of reproduction of labor power. While this theoretically seems to be different from Shaikh's approach, if implies the same thing as far as the calculation of "net tax" (distribution losses of workers in Shaikh's study) is concerned. This method is also consistent with Suzanne de Brunhoff's account of not including the payments to the poor as part of the total value of labor power (de Brunhoff 1976).[4]

Bowles and Gintis' measurement systematically underestimates taxes paid by the working class and overestimates benefits received by them. The very significant "citizen wage" of Bowles and Gintis' study (59 percent of gross earnings of workers or about 40 percent of national income) has not been achieved by the working class and may not be achievable in a capitalist society. It is interesting to note that using their results from Table 3, the sum of wages and "citizen wage" in 1977 accounts for almost all national output leaving nothing for private capital and the state.

Notes

1. A detailed analysis of this issue is presented in chapter four.
2. The original work by Anwar Shaikh (1978) has initiated several other studies in this line. These include Tonak 1984, Fazeli and Fazeli 1984, Bakker 1986, Tonak 1987, Shaikh and Tonak 1987.
3. For durther detail on the method applied in these two studies, see Shaikh and Tonak 1987 and Tonak 1984.
4. In a more recent study, Shaikh and Tonak (1987) have used a broader concept of the working class which also includes the recipients of Public Assistance and Welfare. This item is, therefore, counted as the benefit received by the working population. However, this has not resulted in any significant change in the trend of net social wage for the United States.

4 The welfare state and the reproduction of the working population: The study of the social wage in the United Kingdom

I. Theories of the welfare state and their empirical evaluation

Our major concern in this research is with the impact of social policy on British society and particularly on the British working population. The literature on social policy has paid attention to three major aspects of social policy consequences. The first aspect is the implication of social policy on economic growth. The main question to be addressed is whether the expansion of social welfare programs encourage or undermine economic growth. The second aspect of the debate has to do with the ways in which social policy contributes to political stability and instability. The third is concerned with the contribution of the welfare state to the satisfaction of need, the achievement of a minimum standard of living in society, and reduced inequality. We start this Chapter by a brief review and analysis of the literature on the impact of social policy. We have discussed these issues in some details in the context of the previous Chapters. Our objective in this Chapter is to provide a more direct and explicit presentation of the debate on the effects of social policy in order to identify more clearly the relevance and contribution of our own empirical study.

Social policy has always been seen as having a significant role to play in inducing social and political stability. As we discussed in Chapter one, such an idea was an important factor in the development of the Elizabethan Poor Law. From a Durkheimian perspective, the welfare state can be understood as an attempt to create a new kind of solidarity and integration in the highly differentiated capitalist societies (Flora-Heidenheimer, 1982: 24.) The contribution of social services to social and political integration has also been central to Beveridge's thinking. The intent of the

Post-War development of the welfare state in Britain was to make the liberal market society not only economically more stable and productive but also more stable and harmonious politically (Mishra, 1984: 6,7). The concern with stability and harmony was a main theme in Titmuss's famous work, *The Gift Relationship* (Titmuss, 1970). Mishra suggests that Marshall follows the same theme by emphasizing "the part that social services can play in creating and maintaining solidarity in conditions of modern society" (Mishra, 1981: 35). The idea of political stability is also an important part of the Marxian theory of the welfare state. Various Marxist writers, such as O'Connor (1973), Offe(1987), Gough (1979), and Wolfe(1977), have stressed that welfare programs play an important role in promoting the political legitimacy of the capitalist state and the capitalist mode of production.

There are other authors who pay attention to the more concrete aspects of social policy and specific social programs and the role they play in maintaining social and political stability. George and Wilding (1984: 189) suggest that by easing of social problems and reducing suffering, the welfare state "appears as benevolent and caring, not concerned simply for profit, growth and order, but as concerned, too, for individual citizens and their needs. The established order assumes a new legitimacy and so attracts new sources of loyalty". Doyal (1979:43) stresses the same theme in his evaluation of the role of health services. In his view, "the provision of medical care often comes to represent the benevolent face of an otherwise unequal and divided society." Disney (1982) lays emphasis on the role that unemployment insurance plays in promoting an individualistic ideology. "Unemployment insurance programs in most western countries (writes Disney) embody an individualistic conception of eligibility, requiring individual contribution conditions or means testing of personal income and wealth which both stems from and reinforces social conceptions of unemployment as an individual experience resulting from personal failure in a competitive labor market" (Disney, 1982:25). Thus social policy operates on the basis that claimants are in need because of individual factors and not as the result of the working of the economic system.

The same principle is applied to other social services. The policy of providing housing is based on the assumption that the causes of homelessness lie in the characteristics of individuals rather than the operation of the housing market in a capitalist society. The assumption is that normal people should face no problem in providing for their housing needs. The National Health Service is based on an individualized definition of illness rather than on an environmental view. As Navrro (1976:207) suggests: "the ideology of medicine was the individualization of a collective causality that by its very nature would have required a collective answer." Other authors have argued that social programs support authority and hierarchy in society. This is particularly argued for the case of the educational system. George and Wilding (1984: 206) argue that schools "teach the virtue of achievement, individualism, hard work, respect for authority, the inevitability of inequality and so on." Bourdieu writes: "by making social hierarchies and the reproduction of these hierarchies appear to be based upon the hierarchy of gifts, merits or skills ... the education system fulfills a function of legitimating which is more and more necessary to the perpetuation of the social order ... "(See George and Wilding, 1984: 212).

In spite of all positive contributions of social welfare programs to political and social stability, the legitimacy of the welfare state itself has been challenged in recent decades. Welfare states in Western Europe and North America have run into economic difficulties in the 1970's and 1980's. The economic growth which made state expenditures relatively cost free and painless has ended. The ending of growth has opened up more debates about the legitimacy of the state intervention and particularly the social policy. There are two major groups of theories identifying a deep crisis or at least the potential for such a crisis in welfare capitalism: the neoconservative thesis of the "government overload" and the "state contradiction" thesis developed by Marxian authors.

The proponents of the overload in government thesis argue that governments in the era of welfare capitalism are overloaded with duties and responsibilities far beyond their capacity to deliver and they see this as threatening to the political stability and the legitimacy of the welfare state and welfare capitalism. The best known representatives of this approach are King (1975) and Brittan (1975). King defines the problem in terms of administrative overload, while Brittan identifies the problem more as a system overload.

For King government overload resulted from the increasing complexity of its role in society. The division of labor, the increase in standards of living, and the increases in the scale and complexity of international trade lead to structural changes in society which in turn put pressure on governments to expand the range and the scale of their activities. Governments, on the other hand, lack the necessary resources to perform these multiple duties.

For Brittan the source of the problem is the nature of the democratic process which leads to excessive expectations by the voters. From his point of view, the democratic process operates as a political markets in which competing parties and interest groups strive to outdo each other in their promises to satisfy the rising expectations of the voters. Such a competitive democracy induces the perception that everything is possible. In this way the system is overloaded with more and more activities of the government in response to immediate demands without taking into account the availability of resources. However, this system of rising expectations and increasing scale of state intervention requires an economic mode of justification. This economic rationale is provided by Keynesianism. On the basis of the Keynesian theory, increased government expenditure induces economic activities which lead to the generation of more revenue for government. At the same time the universal acceptance of Keynesian economic policy leads to the repudiation of the balanced budget as the apparent sign of financial responsibility of the government.

Both Brittan and King foresee the possibility of a crisis of the regime in such dimensions that Britain has not experienced for a long period of time. They do not present any clear idea as to how this crisis can be avoided. They both see the possibility of a movement toward a more "authoritative government." King is more specific in this regard. He predicts a situation in which the citizens lose their power to government and govern gains power but loses authority. In other words, government is moving away from democracy and party competition toward a situation in which it increasingly loses its legitimate authority and has to exercise more coercion to restore the crisis.

We now turn to discuss the empirical validity of the overload theory. We may draw certain hypotheses from the overload theory that can be empirically tested. The overload thesis suggests that competitive political markets lead to the over expansion of public expenditures. If we follow the rationale of this thesis, we should expect that the articulated demands of pressure groups and the electorate to be concerned predominantly with the issues of social security and the provision of social services. Thus, the share of social expenditures in public expenditures should rise over time. On the other hand, government overload results when demands for public expenditures exceed the resources available to government. This means that a widening gap between total public expenditures and revenues will evolve over time. The increased budget deficit should be primarily directed toward financing rising social expenditures. We should also expect that the increase in social expenditures to be less a function of economic growth and to be instead determined by political factors. In fact, if anything, the demand for some social expenditures, such as unemployment insurance and welfare expenditures, should increase in the recessionary period. Finally, the overload theory implies that the competitive democratic process will lead to the increased demand of the public (primarily the working population) for social services. The working population is not only interested in receiving a higher gain from social services but also in receiving a higher level of after tax wage. This means that the net social wage, which is defined to be the difference between benefits received by workers from state activities and taxes paid by them to government, should increase over time.

There are certain structural similarities between neoconservative theories of "ungovernability" of the state and the radical critique of the welfare state. The limits of growth of the welfare state, the crisis of legitimating or the crisis of the authority of the state have become more or less standard topics. Radicals agree with neoconservatives about some form of overload and the widening gap between state expenditures and taxes which, in their view, leads to the "fiscal crisis of the state." However, the former theorists see the cause of the crisis as rooted in the inherent contradictions of the capitalist economic system. There are several major contributions: O'Connor (1973), Gough (1979), Wolfe (1977), and Offe (1987).

The main thesis is most clearly developed by O'Connor who argues the state in a capitalist society must "try to fulfill two basic and often mutually contradictory functions - accumulation and legitimating" in order to contribute to the stability of the economy (p. 6). The state is involved in the accumulation function in order to create the conditions in which private capital remains profitable. The legitimating function is associated with the effort of the state to maintain social harmony.

O'Connor identifies three categories of the state expenditures: social investment, social consumption, and social expenses. Social investment is directed toward those activities which increase labor productivity or lower the costs of private capital. This includes investment in infrastructure and direct subsidies to private business.

Social consumption is designed to lower the reproduction costs of labor power. This includes those state expenditures, such as health, education, and social insurance, which contribute to the reproduction of the working population. Social expenses are those expenditures which contribute to social harmony and fulfill the legitimating function. The primary components of these expenditures are welfare expenses and other expenditures directed toward the maintaining of law and order. The source of crisis is the "socialization of costs and the private appropriation of profits." This is what, writes O'Connor, "creates a fiscal crisis" or "structural gap" between state expenditures and its revenues (p.9).

Gough's treatment of state expenditures is very similar to that of O'Connor. He argues that while all state activities are unproductive, but some contribute either to the reproduction of capital or labor power. He divides state expenditures into three departments: social constant capital, social variable capital, and luxuries. Social constant capital is reproductive because it lowers the production costs of capital. Social variable capital contributes to the reproduction of labor power. The categories of expenditures belonging to the third department are considered to be unreproductive, since they do not contribute either to the reproduction of capital or to the reproduction of labor. These expenditures are directed to maintain law and order or social harmony. The major difference between Gough and O'Connor on the contradictory development and the crisis of the welfare state is that Gough pays more attention to class struggle as a major component of the theory of the state. This aspect of Gough's analysis has been discussed in Chapter two and there is no need to reproduce it here.

Offe's state contradiction thesis is of substantial resemblance to O'Connor's model. Offe argues that an important source of illegitimacy and crisis of the welfare state is its chronic fiscal problem. Fiscal deficit is continuously growing because there is a contradiction between the increasing costs of the welfare state's "socialization" of production and the continuing private control over investment and the appropriation of profit. In other words, the viability of economic growth depends on the ability of the welfare state to subsidize capital and to provide social services required for the reproduction of labor power. But, on the other hand, the state's ability to finance these rising expenditures is dependent upon the prosperity and continued profitability of private capital.

Offe explains this basic contradiction as one between commodification and decommodification roles of the state. On the one hand, the welfare state must promote commodity production and private accumulation of capital and, on the other hand, the maintenance and generalization of private exchange relations depends upon decommodified policies which are required to promote continuous investment of capital and the commodification of the labor power. In a word, welfare state policies are expected to do the impossible. For Offe the New Right defense of "re-privatization" does not provide a valid solution for the crisis, because it is self-contradictory. He argues that the frontiers of the welfare state can not be "rolled back". Capitalist economies can not continue to function successfully without the continuous state provision of social services, since they are required for both private accumulation of capital and the legitimating of the state.

Wolfe follows O'Connor's ideas and incorporates in his analysis the political contradictions of the democratic welfare state. He defines the main contradiction of capitalist societies as a continuing and intensifying conflict between liberal and democratic aspects of the state. In his analysis liberal political arrangements are associated with the need to facilitate accumulation and to legitimate the economic system of capitalism. The democratic trend is, on the other hand, the product of the increasing requirement of the system to promote social and political legitimating and to maintain popular acceptance and loyalty. It is the contradiction between these two aspects, mediated through class struggle, which cause the fundamental crisis of welfare capitalism. The struggle of the working class makes it impossible for the state to resolve the contradiction in favor of private capital and accumulation. The state is required to expand its activities to aid accumulation, but it must at the same time spend more on welfare and social control to secure its legitimacy. In this process, "the more the state does ... the less it can do" (p.247). "Damned if it does and damned if it doesn't the state approaches the point at which its utility for reproducing social relations is nil" (p.259).

The "state contradiction theories" are more complex than the "overload" model of the welfare state crisis. It may be more difficult to capture the essence of these theories in an empirical study. It is, nevertheless, possible to develop a similar hypotheses based on these theories. The expanding requirement of welfare capitalism to safeguard legitimating and social harmony implies an increased demand for welfare expenditures. On the other hand, the accumulation function also requires, in part, an expansion of social expenditures to maintain the reproduction of labor power. This means that the share of social and welfare expenditures in total public expenditures and GNP must go up over time. This trend will also result in a rising budget deficit ("the fiscal crisis of the state") to cover the widening gap between state expenditures and revenues.

The question is whether we can draw any hypothesis with regard to the trend of the net social wage from these theories. There is no clear answer to this question. This is because the tax side of the state activities is mostly neglected. We may suggest that based on these theories, economic recession should result in a tax backlash by the middle class and the working population who are concerned with their diminishing after tax income. On the other hand, the concern of the state with both accumulation and legitimating aspects may make it difficult for the state to carry out drastic cuts in social expenditures. This means that the net social wage should increase over time and result in an exacerbation of the budgeting crisis of the welfare state. We will see that the results of our study do not fully confirm the above hypothesis. As we discussed in Chapters two and three, Bowles and Gintis (1980) have developed a model of the crisis of welfare capitalism which is based on the class struggle. Their empirical study is based on the evidence for the case of the United State. They use this study to support a rather universal claim on the rise in the "citizen wage" which is in their view responsible for the crisis of welfare capitalism. This idea is also important because it is used as an integral part of "the Social Structure of Accumulation" model which has become an influential trend in recent years (see Bowles, Gordon, and Weisskopf, 1989).

The question of whether capitalism is still capitalism and whether the state is still a capitalist state depends in large part on how we address two major questions about the role of the state in contemporary society; its role in production and its role in distribution. In this work we are primarily concerned with the second question: the distribution impact of social policy. The question we address is whether the state has adopted policies to modify the patterns of class inequality and differential reward, produced by property relations and the market structure of a capitalist economy. Our country of study is the United Kingdom, but the empirical findings will have theoretical implications not only for the United Kingdom but also for other advanced capitalist societies.

II. Empirical methodology

Studies on the welfare state and social policy have generally concentrated on the expenditures side of state activities and have paid no or little attention to the impact of taxes on benefit recipients. Their emphasis even on the expenditures side has been mostly on those state activities which are directly applied as the means of social policy, such as social transfer payments and social expenditures, neglecting the redistributive contribution of other publicly provided commodities and services, such as transportation, communication, public utilities, and so forth. Other studies by public economists, while taking into account both the effect of expenditures and taxes, have been concerned with the redistributive implications of state activities for different income groups and not the working population.

There are also major methodological differences between these studies and the present research. The methodology adopted in the standard studies (see Chapter three) is based on the assumption of equal effective use among all individuals of a particular category (of given sex and age) of publicly provided goods such as education and health. This assumption is supposedly consistent with the principle of "universality"[1] of social services. It has been generally believed that if services are made available free to all, then they will be used by everyone who needs them. In other words, it is assumed that all individuals or households have equal access to social services. Thus, 'universality' is identified with equality of use. However, this assumption is bound to be at odds with the realities of a society in which differences in class, gender, and racial status can lead to differential market rewards.

In this study, we are assuming that benefits received by different households and individuals from public goods and services are not of the same magnitude. The wealthier households living in the more prosperous areas may have better access to social services and may also benefit from goods and services of better quality. We will discuss the methodology we have adopted for this purpose and its more detailed justification in the following sections.

The working population as a whole receives benefits from state expenditures and pays taxes. The net aggregate benefit or tax depends on the amount of benefits received and taxes paid by the whole population of workers' families. In order to identify the net benefit/burden position of the working population in relation to state activities, we principally apply the methodology developed by

Shaikh (1978), with certain modifications to make it compatible with the British national accounting system. The benefits received by working population families from state expenditures will be called 'social benefits' in order to distinguish them from other benefits the workers receive in relation to their employment as part of employees compensation. The difference between social benefits and taxes paid by workers is a net transfer which we call the "net social wage". In this book, a broad concept of the working class is adopted which includes all wage earners.

In a separate measurement of the net social wage, the labor of the self-employed and unpaid family labor is also taken into account. It is thus reasonable to consider proprietors and partners in non-corporate business as part workers and part owners. We will therefore attempt to split their income into wage equivalent and profit equivalent components. (See Appendix II for the results of this separate measurement). This is particularly true because in most cases the self-employed are unable to accumulate a large amount of capital and in this way their potential chance to become members of the capitalist class or the elite is not substantial. It may be safe to assume that the self-employed would have certain common interests with other members of the working population, particularly with regard to welfare measures, such as social security, welfare expenditures, the public provision of health and educational services, and so forth.

In a different account, the results for the net social wage will be adjusted to exclude the share of top managers in both benefits and taxes. While the members of this group occupy a contradictory location between capital and labor, they are much closer to the former. Since they exercise a large degree of control over the production process and the process of decision-making, they are also able to receive substantially higher salaries than ordinary workers which are in part concealed profits. However, they have the ability to accumulate which means that their income is comprised of not only salaries but also income from other sources such as investment and capital gain. It is thus reasonable to exclude this group from the working population and consider them as an integral part of the bourgeoisie. The trend of the net social wage adjusted to take into account the share of top managers will be presented in Appendix III.

1. The role of the state expenditures

The expenditure categories of the welfare state can be classified into three groups. It is useful to use some benchmark against which to measure changes in expenditures over time. Absolute changes in expenditures, measured in money terms, can be misleading. This is because both price levels and money incomes have continually increased for the period of our study.

We are using three different benchmarks: GNP, total expenditures, and labor income. GNP is the benchmark which is most commonly used. An increase of the proportion of state expenditures in GNP is indicative of the growing importance of these expenditures and also a possible diversion of resources from the private sector to the public sector. The rise of categories of expenditure as the proportion of total expenditures implies the increasing weight of this item in public policy. Using this benchmark allows us to evaluate the empirical validity of the theories of the welfare state crisis which we explained in the first section of this Chapter. Finally, the benchmark of labor income is used to determine the changing importance of each category of expenditures in the consumption of the working population.

Table 4.1 includes the data on the expenditure categories for selected years in the post-war period. The value of state expenditures are presented both in absolute terms and as a percentage of GNP. Throughout the following sections, the share of each expenditure category as a proportion of total state expenditures and labor income will be shown in separate Figures. Tables 1 and 2 in Appendix I demonstrate how the net social wage and the contribution of each expenditure category to the net social wage is measured. We now proceed to present the analysis of each group of state expenditures and the method of the measurement of the net social wage.

Before moving to the next section on the methodology of this study, it may be appropriate to address the question of the definition of the "social wage" and the "net social wage." John Harrison suggests that "the use of "social wage" is clearly intended to indicate that the receipt of the state benefits included in the notion is in some way equivalent to the receipt of wages" (Harrison, 1980: 384)

The question is whether we should include both benefits in cash and in kind in the notion of "social wage" or to define the concept as only the cash payment from the state to the working population. In his analysis of the data on the flows between the personal and state sector, Gough defines "social wage" as the "return flow of state benefits and services back to the capitalist or marketed sector" (Gough, 1979: 108). In another context, when he is discussing the role of welfare state policies on accumulation, he argues that "it may be preferable to restrict the term social wage to the group of cash benefits and call the benefits in kind 'collective consumption' " (p.116).

However this second concept of "social wage" is questionable. Gough does not provide any further explanation for this second notion of "social wage". But it seems that his argument is based on the proposition that only benefits in cash contribute to money wages (or market wages) of the working population and as such constitute wages. But money wages are the monetary expression of the value of the labor power which is equivalent to the value of the commodities entering into the normal consumption of the working population household. To exclude the "collective consumption" from "social wage" or wage will bring about a significant discrepancy between the value of labor power and wage which is unjustifiable on theoretical grounds.

In this research, we define "social wage" as benefits received either in cash or in kind by the working population from all different categories of state expenditures. The "net social wage" will be defined as the difference between benefits received and taxes paid by the working population.

We now proceed to explain the methodology of measurement of the state expenditures in this book. State expenditures are classified in three groups: the direct payment of cash benefits and subsidies in cash and kind, the direct provision of commodities and services in relation to social policy, and the indirect benefits accrued to workers by general public provision of goods and services.

Group I The first group includes, in large part, transfer payments whose function is income maintenance for phases of unemployment or underemployment in the life cycle of the working population, such as maternity, old age, and widowhood; cases of incapacity in employment, such as sickness, injuries, invalidity, and unemployment. This group also includes certain other benefits in cash and kind, such as Public Assistance supplementing income maintenance programs.

In our categorization in Table 4.1 and tables 1 and 2 in Appendix I, these items are presented in a more aggregate form. These categories include Social Security Benefits and Public Assistance and Welfare.

Table 4.1
Public expenditures trends

Year	1953	% of GNP	1960	% of GNP	1965	% of GNP	1970	% of GNP	1975	% of GNP	1980	% of GNP	1986	% of GNP
Group I														
Social Security Benefits	528	3.49	996	4.36	1783	5.63	2731	6.19	6432	6.75	14689	7.59	25131	7.68
Public Assistance and Welfare	478	3.16	635	2.78	857	2.71	1618	3.67	3855	4.05	10162	5.25	25064	7.66
Transfer Payments	1006	6.66	1631	7.13	2640	8.34	4349	9.86	10287	10.80	24851	12.85	50195	15.34
Group II														
Housing	569	3.77	490	2.14	957	3.02	1319	2.99	4459	4.68	6171	3.19	4195	1.28
Education	457	3.02	890	3.89	1480	4.67	2423	5.49	6453	6.77	12753	6.59	19521	5.96
Health	529	3.50	879	3.84	1303	4.11	2031	4.60	5272	5.54	11629	6.01	19446	5.94
Social Expenditures	2561	16.95	3890	17.01	6380	20.15	10122	22.94	26471	27.79	55404	28.64	93357	28.52
Group III														
Public Utilities, Recreation	142	0.94	241	1.05	400	1.26	612	1.39	1051	1.10	3687	1.91	10183	3.11
Transport, Communication, Public Roads, and Lighting	298	1.97	739	3.23	1025	3.24	983	2.23	2434	2.56	3409	1.76	3681	1.12
(Contributory) Civil Public Consumption	1995	8.72	3239	14.16	5165	16.31	7368	16.70	19669	20.65	37649	19.46	57026	17.42
Gross National Product	15110		22870		31667		44128		95248		193450		327300	

Note: 'Transfer Payments' is the sum of categories in group I. 'Social Expenditures' is the sum of group I and group II. 'Contributory Civil Public Consumption' is defined as those items in Civil Public Consumption contributing to the benefit of the working population. It is the sum of all categories in group II and III.

82

These two forms of expenditure together constitute the transfer payments. Figure 4.1 shows the share of transfer payments in total state expenditures and in the GNP. The share of transfer payments in GNP has steadily but slowly increased over time. This ratio has increased from less than 7 percent in 1953 to about 15 percent in 1986. The faster growth of this ratio between 1973 and 1982 can be explained better when we look at Figures 6.2 and 6.4. The recent increase in the amount of transfer payments has been primarily due to the rise of Public Assistance and Welfare. This item absorbed only 3 percent of GNP up to 1968, but it has achieved more significance in recent years. In 1986 Public Assistance constituted close to 8 percent of GNP. This change can be explained by the rising rate of unemployment, structural change in industry, and population change.

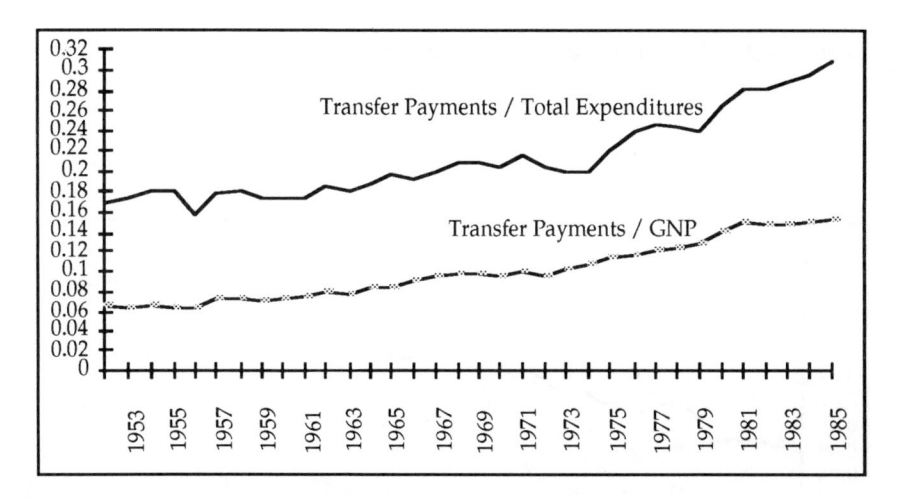

Figure 4.1 The share of transfer payments in total expenditures and in GNP

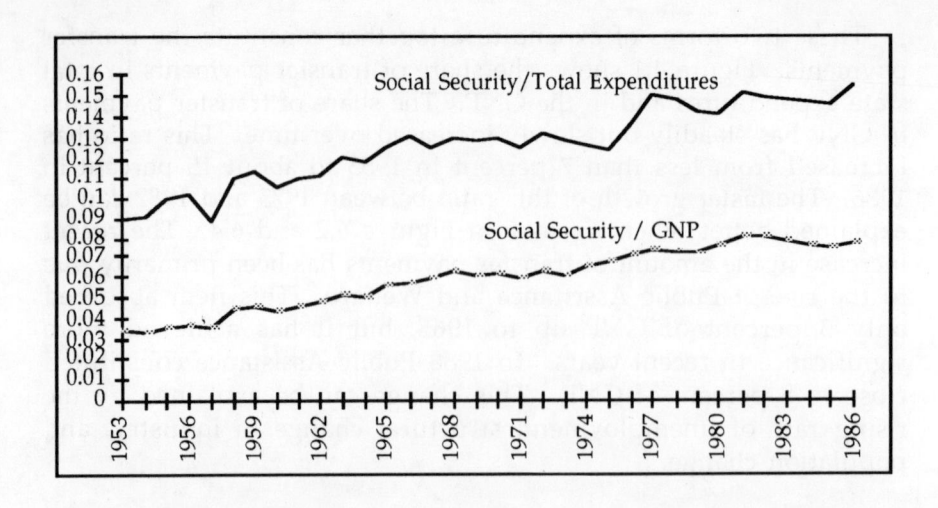

Figure 4.2 The share of social security in total expenditures

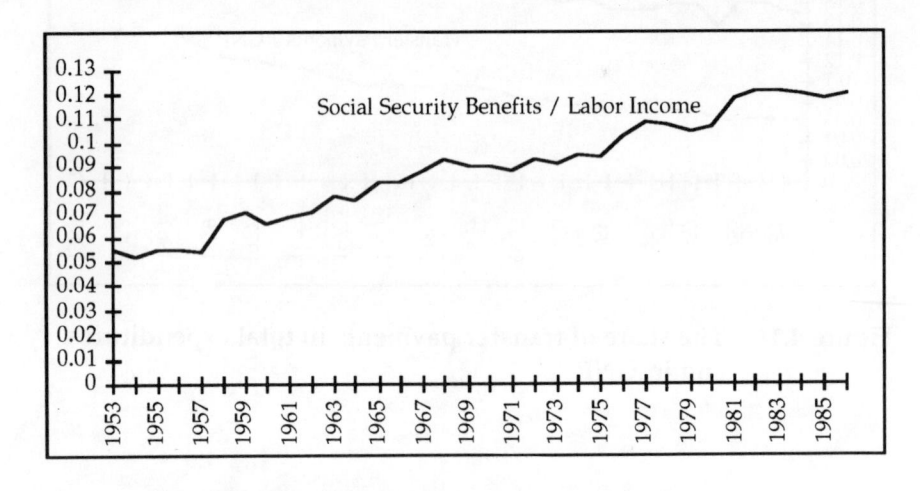

Figure 4.3 The share of social security in labor income

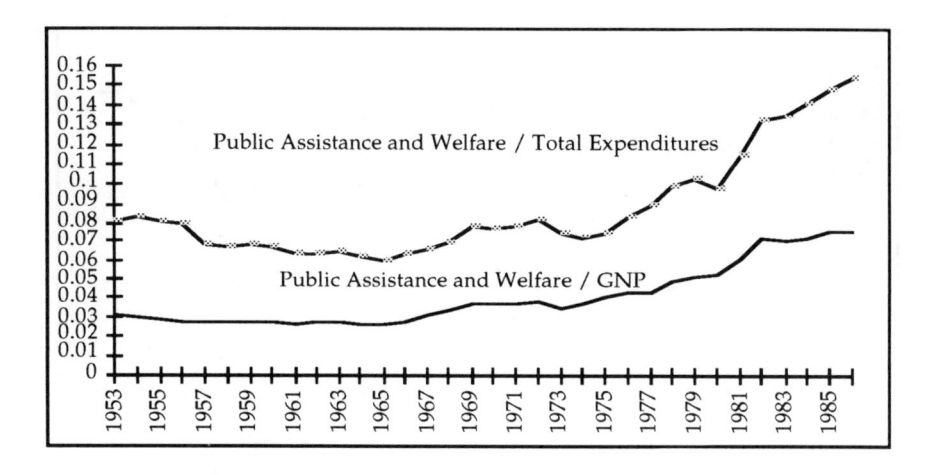

Figure 4.4 The share of public assistance and welfare in total expenditures and in GNP

The unemployment rate remained low throughout the 1950's and 1960's. But from 1975 on it rose substantially. During the period of 1979-86, the average rate of unemployment has been close to 12 percent (see Table 4.3). The continuation of the high unemployment rate has led not only to higher expenditures on unemployment benefits but also a higher cost of supplementary benefits and other welfare expenditures. The growth of the dependent population (children and elderly) and the rise in the proportion of low paying jobs in the service sector and government have also contributed to the rising costs of welfare and public assistance. In recent years the total wages received by workers have been far below what is required to reproduce the entire working population (see Figure 4.5).

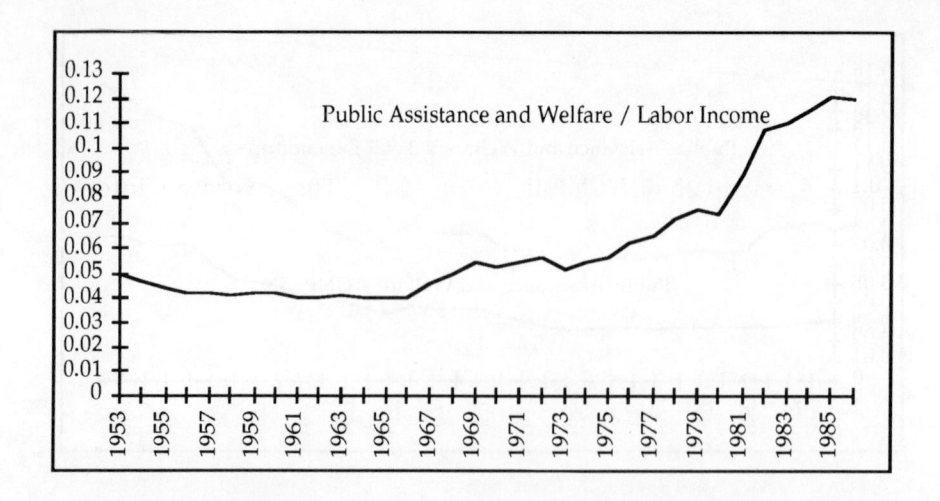

Figure 4.5 The share of public assistance and welfare in labor income

The measurement of the net social wage for a sample year is presented in tables 1 and 2 in Appendix I. The first category of this group, Social Security, is assumed to be received as a whole by workers and their families. The inclusion of social security as a whole leads to some overestimation as well. We have excluded the military old age and disability payments from this category on the ground that military service men are not members of the working class. But some non-funded items like judges' and tax court retirement funds are included in this category and can not be excluded out. These, however, are probably of no significant value.

The second item, Public Assistance and Welfare, includes, for the most part, payments to and publicly provided commodities and services consumed by the poor. O'Connor (1973) identified these state expenditures as "social expenses," the function of which is to maintain social harmony and the legitimacy of the state. However, total separation of welfare expenses from the conditions for the reproduction of labor and perceiving them as acting only to legitimize the state, is not appropriate. Marx calls pauperism "...the hospital of the active labor army and the dead weight of the industrial reserve army." While it constitutes the incidental costs of capitalist production, yet "along with the surplus population, pauperism forms a condition of capitalist production, and of the capitalist development of wealth" (Marx 1977: 603). The same process which generates the industrial reserve army, leads to the creation of pauperism. T.H. Marshall has also characterized the paupers of the nineteenth century as those separated from the working class: "The paupers were not a social class, in the sense which implies a particular role or situation in the socioeconomic system, because they had fallen out of it. They were an inferior status group, marked by loss of legal rights and social status. It was their dependency, not their poverty, which determined their classification as paupers" (Marshall 1981: 41, 42).

In the Poor Law period only the "paupers" were clearly recognized as the poor who were eligible to receive public assistance, although in the repressive and degrading form of poor relief. Relief was granted to those who were desperate enough to give up their independent status and citizenship rights and "cross the road that separated the community of citizens from company of the destitute" (Marshall 1964: 81). In the era of the welfare state this concept of poverty has been, to some extent, transformed. The recipients of Public Assistance include not only those who have lost the independent means of earning an income, or those who have fallen out of the net of the social insurance system, but also those whose earnings are not adequate to maintain a minimum subsistence and are consequently entitled to receive some form of assistance, such as family income supplement or family allowance. The poor, in other words, include those separated from the labor force, who are forced to live on the margin of society, and those who, while working, receive such low pay that they can not maintain their subsistence at a level above the officially defined poverty line.

There are two major programs providing public assistance for the poor or low paid workers: supplementary benefits and family allowances. Supplementary benefits was initially designed to be paid only to the elderly. Its scope was gradually expanded to cover a larger population. In the recent decades, the family income supplement has become a means to supplement the family income of low wage earners. It is recognized that only families whose standards of living are below the officially defined poverty line are eligible to receive a family income supplement. The government supplement is half the difference between the family's gross income and the prescribed amount. This procedure is based on the belief that generous government supplements can have a negative effect on workers' incentive to work. As George (1973: 680) has stated, "the family income supplement is a blatant social class policy measure designed to reduce government expenditure and openly admitting that allowing people to live in poverty is not unreasonable."

The second social policy program providing assistance to families is family allowance. The aim of this program is to provide allowance to all families with children. This scheme, however, is progressive, since it provides more benefits to lower income groups than the higher income groups. There is no allowance for the first child and the net benefit of the allowance goes down as the families income increases. This is because the family allowance is taxable.

Nevertheless, it should be noted that alongside this program, there are child tax allowances from which higher income families benefit more than lower income families. Child tax allowances exempt a certain amount of the family's income from taxation for each dependent child. Families with more children are, therefore, exempted from taxation for a higher amount of income. This means that higher income families benefit from a larger amount of tax relief than the lower income families considering the fact that the tax system is nominally progressive in the United Kingdom.

The decision to include Public Assistance and Welfare as the share of the working class in social benefits would depend on our characterization of the working class and the objective of the study. A large part of the poor remains separated from the labor force and the main production relations in capitalist society. Hence, it would be safe to assume a large portion of Public Assistance and Welfare is not directly consumed by the working class. But this ratio has not remained constant over time. The increased number of low pay jobs, the rise in the number of single-parent families, and the lower wages paid to women and immigrant workers have led to the enlargement of the Public Assistance received by the working poor in the last two decades. In this book we will, therefore, present two sets of results: one without inclusion of this category as the share of labor and the second with this item included (see Table 1 in Appendix I).

Group II The second group includes the provision of goods and services, such as Education, Health Services, and Public Housing. These expenditures are closely connected with state intervention in markets such as housing or the supply of health services. In public finance theory, these commodities and services are characterized as quasi-public goods due to significant externalities associated with them. Spending on Public Housing has fluctuated in the post-war period but it has continuously declined in recent years. (see Figures 4.6 and 4.7) The cut-back in housing expenditure started under the last Labor government and continued on a larger scale under the Thatcherite conservative government (see tables 4.2 and 4.3). This trend reflects a shift in public policy from public provision of housing to its market supply. As Figure 4.7 shows the contribution of public housing for the consumption of the working population has declined.

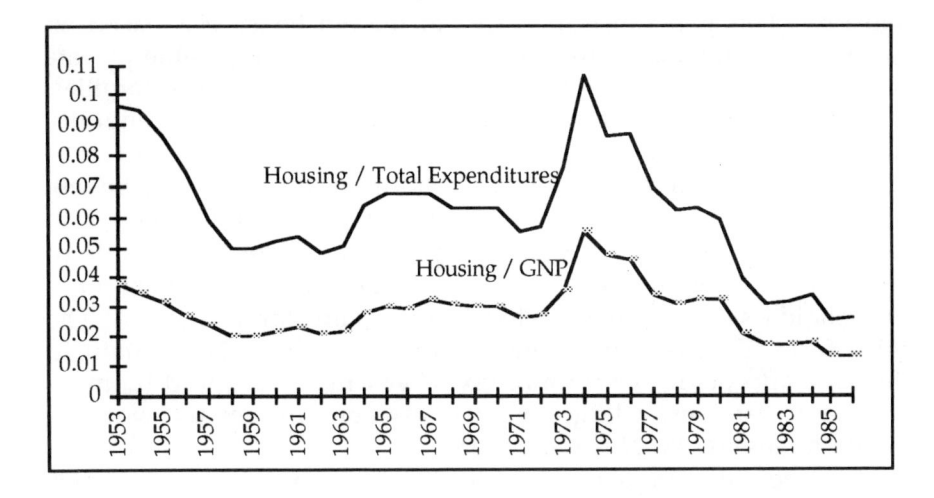

Figure 4.6 The share of housing in total expenditures and in GNP

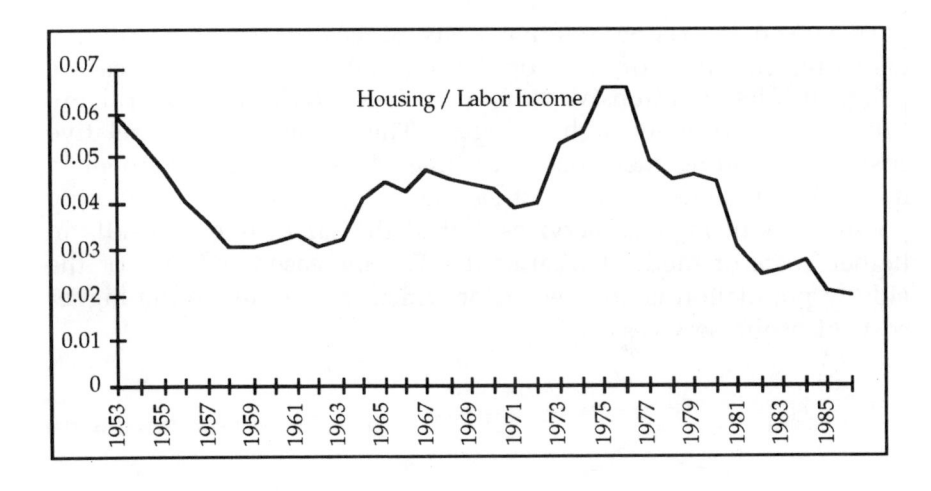

Figure 4.7 The share of housing in labor income

Public Housing is in a large part used by the working population. In our measurement of the labor share, the whole expenditures on Public Housing are allocated to the working class. The benefits recorded are only the subsidies of the government in the case of local authorities' housing which is also called Council Housing. The tenants of the dwellings pay lower than market rents. The actual amount of benefits received by tenants exceeds the amount of subsidy. This is because the value of the old housing is based on historic cost rather than the current value of the comparable private housing. The benefit is not always received by the poorest families. Average local authority household income has been generally higher than that of privately rented accommodation. But it is reasonable to assume that the vast majority of these families belong to the working population. The second group of families who benefit from the housing policy of government are the tenants of controlled accommodations. The amount of rent that these households save is not reflected in the figure for this item. The third form of housing is owner-occupied housing. The benefit in this case appears in the form of tax relief which is enjoyed by more well-to-do families, a large number of whom are not the working class families (see Webb 1971: 49-54).

The spending on health has steadily risen over time (see tables 4.2 and 4.3). The government has increasingly allocated more resources to Health (Figure 4.8). This moderate increase in expenditures on Health does not necessarily imply any considerable improvement in the quality of health care for the working population. The relative rise of Health expenditures has been in part caused by rising relative costs of health services and the changing structure of the population. Since health services are primarily labor intensive, there is less possibility of raising productivity to offset higher wages. This means that the relative costs of providing them rise over time. Even the improvement in medical technology is not cost saving. It increases the life-saving possibilities of medical services, but at the same time it results in higher costs of medical treatment. The increased number of the elderly population is another factor which contributes to the higher costs of health services.

Table 4.2

Periodization of public expenditures programs

Period	Average Annual Percentage Rate of Increase						Adjusted for Inflation					
	1953-57	1957-64	1964-70	1970-74	1974-79	1979-86	1953-57	1957-64	1964-70	1970-74	1974-79	1979-86
(1) Defense and External Relations	-1.18	4.00	3.53	14.16	17.37	9.58	-4.82	1.37	-1.19	3.18	1.82	1.47
(2) Trade, Industry, Agriculture, and Employment Services	8.67	5.70	8.82	9.84	13.44	1.53	5.03	3.05	4.10	-1.13	-2.11	-6.58
(3) Administration Expenses and Others	5.56	0.00	12.22	21.76	16.66	7.94	1.92	1.99	7.50	10.78	1.11	-0.17
(4) Police, Prison, and Fire	0.28	6.68	10.81	17.68	19.14	12.58	-3.36	4.02	6.09	6.71	3.59	4.47
(5) Social Security Benefits	7.46	11.44	10.47	16.09	19.47	11.04	3.82	8.79	5.75	5.12	3.92	2.93
(6) Public Assistance and Welfare	3.33	5.67	12.41	15.07	25.04	16.37	-0.31	3.02	7.69	4.10	9.49	8.26
(7) Housing	-4.67	8.16	8.38	33.65	4.95	-3.44	-8.31	5.50	3.66	22.68	-10.60	-11.55
(8) Education	11.72	9.38	10.46	16.52	18.21	9.55	8.08	6.73	5.74	5.55	2.66	1.43
(9) Health	7.21	7.45	9.85	18.02	18.18	11.49	3.57	4.79	5.13	7.04	2.63	3.38
(10) Public Utilities, Recreation	7.69	9.74	8.95	10.34	27.27	18.91	4.05	7.08	4.23	-0.64	11.72	10.80
(11) Transport, Communication, Public Roads, and Lighting	14.38	8.83	1.07	19.37	10.18	1.84	10.74	6.17	-3.65	8.40	-5.37	-6.28
(12) Interest, Capital Consumption and Others	0.00	5.19	3.01	26.98	19.73	9.67	0.00	2.53	-1.71	16.00	4.18	1.55
(13) Total Expenditure	0.054	0.062	0.119	0.113	0.171	0.124	0.018	0.035	0.072	0.003	0.015	0.043

A Chronology of Government
- 1953-1957: Conservative Government
- 1957-1964: Conservative Government
- 1964-1974: Labor Government
- 1970-1974: Conservative Government
- 1974-1979: Labor Government
- 1979-1986: Thatcherite Conservative Government

Table 4.3
Post-War cycles (economy and social expenditures)

Cycle	I		II		III		IV		V		VI	
Period	1953-57	Adjusted for Inf.	1957-64	Adjusted for Inf.	1964-70	Adjusted for Inf.	1970-74	Adjusted for Inf.	1974-79	Adjusted for Inf.	1979-86	Adjusted for Inf.
Duration	4years		7years		6years		4years		5years		7years	
Group I												
Social Security Benefits	7.50	3.80	11.40	8.80	10.50	5.70	16.10	5.10	19.50	3.90	11.00	2.60
Public Assistance and Welfare	3.30	-0.30	5.70	3.00	12.40	7.70	15.10	4.10	25.00	9.50	16.40	8.30
Transfer Payments	5.50	1.90	9.10	6.50	11.20	6.40	15.70	4.70	21.60	6.10	13.50	5.30
Group II												
Housing	-4.70	-8.30	8.20	5.50	8.40	3.70	33.70	22.70	4.90	-10.60	-3.40	-11.60
Education	11.70	8.10	9.40	6.70	10.50	5.70	16.50	5.50	18.20	2.70	9.50	1.40
Health	7.20	3.60	7.50	4.80	9.80	5.10	18.00	7.00	18.20	2.60	11.50	3.40
Social Expenditures	5.10	1.50	8.70	6.00	10.30	5.60	19.20	8.20	17.40	1.80	10.80	2.70
Group III												
Public Utilities, Recreation	7.70	4.10	9.70	7.10	8.90	4.20	10.30	-0.60	27.30	11.70	18.90	10.80
Transport, Communication, Public Roads, and Lighting	14.40	10.70	8.80	6.20	1.10	-3.60	19.40	8.40	10.20	-5.40	1.80	-6.30
(Contributory) Civil Public Consumption	6.70	3.00	8.60	5.90	8.20	3.50	20.50	9.50	14.90	-0.70	12.00	3.89
Net Social Wage	-0.70	-4.34	7.98	5.32	-33.29	-38.01	136.01	125.03	-10.62	-26.17	-30.51	-38.63
Unemployment Rate	1.25		2.30		2.40		3.80		5.80		11.50	
Inflation: % Average Annual Rise in Price Index	3.60		2.70		4.70		11.00		15.50		8.10	
Budget Deficit	17.90	14.20	10.20	7.60	-25.40	-30.10	80.20	69.30	11.20	-4.40	-0.80	-8.90
Gross National Product	6.76	3.11	6.05	3.39	6.88	2.16	14.59	3.61	19.50	1.52	10.06	1.95

Note: All measurements are the percent average annual rise in that category except for unemployment. 'Transfer Payment' is the sum of categories in Group I. 'Social Expenditures' is the sum of Group I and Group II. 'Contributory Civil Public Consumption' is the sum of categories in Group II and III.

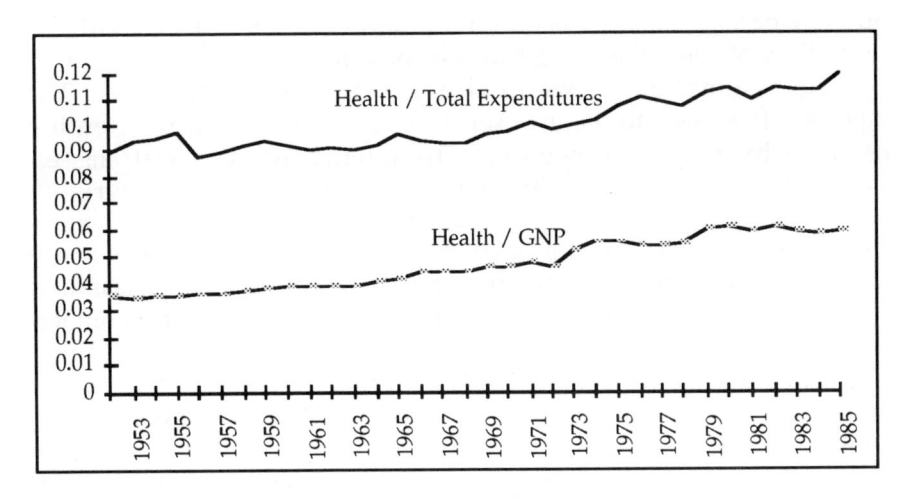

Figure 4.8   The share of health in total expenditures and in GNP

There has also been an improvement in the area of primary care. The number of professional personnel in the National Health Service (NHS) has doubled during 1950-1980. This includes a 26 percent increase in the number of general practitioners and 218 percent in the number of hospital consultants (George and Wilding, 1984: 36). In spite of the increase in the number of general practitioners and other professional personnel, the situation remains less than satisfactory. Patient/staff ratio is still substantially high. There are still 42 percent of practices with more than the generally acceptable standard of 2500 patients per doctor (ibid.: 38). Evidence also indicates that "in six major surgical specialities, 37 percent of patients had been waiting longer than a year, nearly 20 percent for more than two years, and some for four years or more." The improvement in hospital services is more costly because they are the more expensive part of the NHS. They account for 70 percent of total expenditures in one year (Ibid.: 40).

    The question to be addressed now is how to measure the benefits received by the working population from the National Health Service. We may consider two possible methods based on two distinct assumptions with regard to the use of these services by social classes. The first method is to estimate the workers' share in the health services by means of proportion of the working class population in the entire population. This method is based on the assumption of the "universality" of access to health services. In other words, we are assuming equal use by all individuals regardless of their class status and income levels.

This assumption, as we discussed before, is problematic. The degree of access to health services and the medical attention received by families can differ substantially across social classes. There are a number of studies that confirm this point. Cartwright's (1964) study on the geographical distribution of doctors in the early 1960's showed that doctors practicing in the well-to-do areas had a smaller list of patients than the doctors in the working class and poor regions. They were also better trained and had better contacts with hospitals. This means that well-to-do patients had a higher degree of access to doctors and hospitals and enjoyed a higher quality of medical care. Another study by West and Lowe (1976) shows that the availability of general practitioners and health visitors in a given area is inversely correlated with the indicators of need, such as infant mortality rate, and birth rate to mothers aged 15 to 19 years. In other words, those who are in need of a higher degree of medical attention, have a lower degree of access to it. Hart (1975) confirms this finding in his own study. He has conducted a study on medical services in poor industrial areas and affluent areas in which he comes to the conclusion that there is an "inverse care law". This is to say that "the availability of good medical care tends to vary inversely with the need of the population served"(p.205).

George and Wilding (1981) have reviewed a number of studies on uneven geographic distribution of hospital facilities. They arrive at similar results for the differential access to hospitals between poor working class regions and affluent areas. Inner cities and particularly those in London have inferior medical services in terms of general practitioners and surgery facilities. They cite the Minister of Health stating that "very often the best hospital facilities are available where they are least needed" (p.84). The major conclusion that we can draw from these studies and reports is that lower socioeconomic groups have a lower degree of access to general practitioners and hospital facilities and the medical care that they receive is of a poorer quality.

In short, the evidence shows that the assumption of equal access to health care facilities by individuals belonging to different socioeconomic groups is highly questionable. Hence, it is reasonable to assume that the working class families who live in inner city areas and the more humble residential areas receive inferior medical care services. To measure the share of labor in total expenditures on National Health Service, we adopt the methodology first suggested by Shaikh (1980). We assume that the "labor share" is equal to the share of the total labor income in personal income (see tables 1 and 2 in Appendix I for a sample year).

Education spending has steadily increased in the post-war period. But its inflation adjusted rate of growth has considerably declined during the 1970's and 1980's (see Table 4.3). The shares of educational expenditures in total expenditures and GNP which were persistently but slowly rising up to 1975 have recently declined significantly (see Figure 4.9). The last Labor government and the new Conservative administration moved to reduce the relative share of educational expenses. The recent economic slow-down and increased unemployment have squeezed the revenue sources of the government. In the meanwhile they have required the government to spend more on unemployment insurance and welfare. The tax cut policy of the Conservative government has undermined the ability of the government to maintain its expenditures on social services. The conservative ideology of the Thatcher government has also led it to adopt a policy favoring the privatization of the educational system.

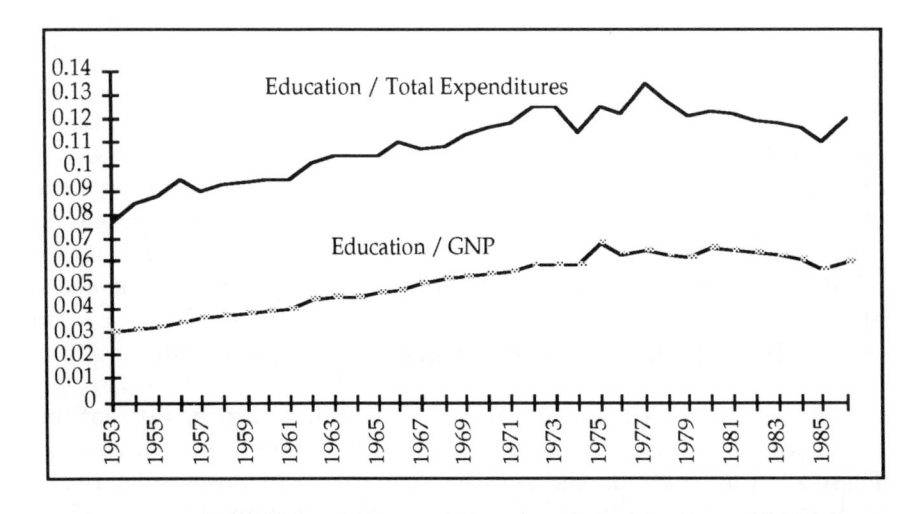

Figure 4.9 The share of education in total expenditures and in GNP

As we discussed earlier, health care benefits were unevenly distributed among socioeconomic groups. A similar pattern can be identified for the case of education. The use of educational facilities has increased for all socioeconomic groups. But this trend should not be confused with increased equality. Evidence shows that inequalities in the use of schooling have changed very little over the last decades. The Newson Report, which was based on a study of secondary schooling, showed that the proportion of seriously inadequate schools was twice as high in the poor areas as compared with the average of the sample (see George and Wilding, 1984:68). The Plowden Report for primary schools concluded that schools in the deprived urban areas were generally older, more overcrowded, less equipped, and more depressing (Ibid.: 68). On the whole, both the quantity and quality of schooling in inner cities, where working class families and minority groups are residing, has been inferior to the middle-class areas.

Halsely et al. (1980) have studied the socioeconomic inequalities in selective higher quality schools. This study concludes that "the likelihood of a working class boy receiving a selective education in the mid-fifties and mid-sixties was very little different from that of his parent's generation thirty years earlier" (p.203). Halsey's study also shows that inequality of use has been even higher at the university level (p.188). One would expect that inequality of use for higher education should have sharpened in recent years due to the reductions in university enrollment introduced by the new Conservative government

The conclusion drawn from the above studies is that the children of the higher income families have a higher degree of access to educational establishments, they attend better schools, and on average stay longer in schools. Thus, the methodology we suggested for the measurement of the benefits of the working population from health services can also be used for the case of education. In other words, we can reasonably assume that the share of the working population in educational services to be proportional to the share of their wages in personal income.

Group III The third group consists of Public Utilities, Recreation, Transportation, Communication, Public Roads, and Lighting. These are public goods and services which are not provided directly as a means of social policy but are partially consumed and used by the working population and consequently affect their standards of living. Past studies on welfare programs as well as those on redistribution, such as Nicholson (1964, 1972) and Stephenson (1976), have tended to neglect this group of expenditures, which contains collective current consumption.

As Figure 4.10 shows the share of public utilities in total expenditures of the government and GNP has slightly increased over time. But transportation and communication have absorbed fewer resources in the last two decades. This trend is similar to that of public investment in the United State. In the U.S. public net investment was as high as 2.3 percent of GNP in 1965-69, but by 1980-84 it had fallen to a mere 0.4 percent.(Heilbroner and Galbraith, 1990: 299) The economic slow-down and the fiscal crisis of the state has led to a cutback in some public expenditures which are politically less sensitive. The decline in public investment causes a parallel decline in the rate of profit on private investment. It may be argued that the deterioration of the infrastructure has partially contributed to higher costs for the private sector and consequently to its lower rate of profit (Ibid.: 300).

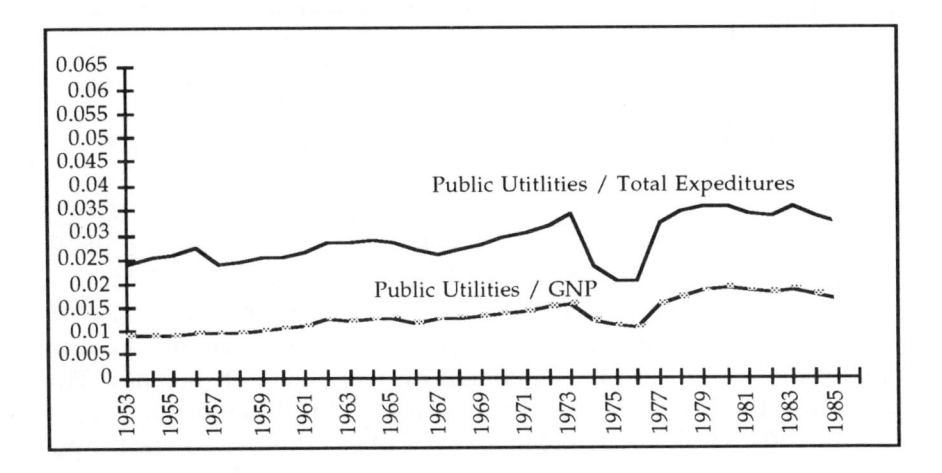

Figure 4.10 The share of public utilities in total expenditures and in GNP

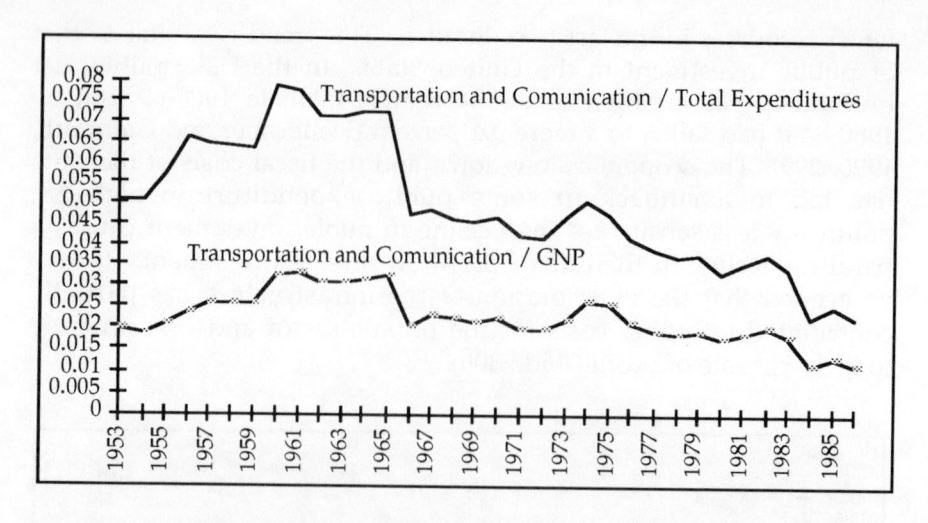

Figure 4.11 The share of transportation and communication in total expenditures and in GNP

There are no comparable studies to evaluate the outcome of the group of expenditures for the working population. It is, however, reasonable to argue that households' consumption of Public Utilities, Recreation, and Transportation and Communication facilities and services are dependent on their level of income. This is because the use of these services requires direct payments or costs for the households. We can expect that households earning a higher level of income to have proportionally a higher demand for these types of facilities and services. Therefore, we treat Public Utilities and Recreation in the same way as Education and Health, as public goods consumed by the household as a whole. The portion allocated to the working population is estimated by multiplying their total value by the labor share.

The other categories in this group: Transportation, Communication, Public Roads, and Lighting, are public goods and services utilized by both the business and the household sectors. Shaikh (1980) has included Communications in the same group as Public Utilities. We suggest that this category should be treated the same way as Transportation, on the grounds that Communication facilities are also consumed by both business and households. For these categories, the household share is first estimated (see tables 1 and 2 in Appendix I), and workers' share is then derived through the "labor share" method. A second set of estimates takes the self-employed into account (see Table 1 in Appendix II). To calculate the share of the households, the total expenditure of this category is multiplied by the ratio of gasoline consumption of passenger cars over the total gasoline consumption. This method was first applied by Musgrave et al. (1974) to measure the share of households in public roads and highways. Shaikh (1980) adopted this method to estimate the share of households in the whole transportation expenditures. This method may result in some overestimation of the household share because the business use of air and water facilities is relatively more than its usage of land transportation.

The remaining group of state expenditures is excluded from labor consumption. It consists of two types: Administration, Legal and Judicial Activities, National Defense, Public Safety and External Relations, which are state expenses contributing to the general reproduction of the system, to the maintenance of the social order and to the reproduction of the state itself (Semmler 1982); and Trade, Industry and Agriculture, Interest, Capital Consumption and Others (unallocables), which directly benefit corporations, small businesses, farmers and high income families. In both studies by Shaikh (1980) and Bowles and Gintis (1980), these items do not constitute any benefits to the working class.

Net interest payments by the government are assumed to be received by capital. For the most part, this is the income of those owning money capital. The working class families may receive part of this as the buyers of government bonds, but this will not be very significant and is not specifically a public benefit received by them. This should essentially be considered as interest income for those who purchase bonds and securities and in this way it is a result of market transactions. If our concern is the total share of the social classes in national output, the inclusion of this item in the benefits received from the state will be double accounting. As far as the state expenditures cost is concerned, this item will be the cost of deficit spending. The share of different categories of the state expenditures will depend on the borrowing requirements of those categories. As an example, social security trust had generally a surplus in the last decades and did not require any borrowing. The other complexity involved is that this item is the cost of deficit spending which is partly initiated by the fiscal policy of the state, the share of social classes on which will depend on the objective and actual effects of the policy. All of these, however, need not be our concern here. The interest received by the working class is not large and it should be counted in the measurement of their general income not as a state benefit received by them. Our assumption is consistent with the two studies by Shaikh and Bowles and Gintis.

2. The impact of taxation

The growing cost of the welfare state has to be financed by one means or another. Government receipts may take three different forms: taxation, trading income (or charges), and borrowing. Taxes and charges are withdrawn from the household or the business without leaving the government with a liability to the private sector. Borrowing, on the other hand, involves an increased liability for the government. The government is expected to repay its debt at a future date and to pay interest in the interim. Taxation has provided the bulk of government finances. Trading income has not constituted a large proportion of government receipts. The substantial rise in state expenditures has not been financed by means of a long-term growth in borrowing requirements until recently. However, in the last decade the budget deficit has risen to a considerable degree. The increased deficit spending has been primarily used to finance the rising cost of the welfare spending resulting from continuing high unemployment.

Tax categories are also classified into three groups. Group one included those taxes which are paid entirely by the workers. These are taxes on wages and salaries, social security and payroll taxes. Both Employees' and Employers' contribution to the Social Insurance Fund are counted as labor taxes. This is because our measure of labor income includes employers' contributions to National Insurance.[2]

Over time direct taxation has increased much faster than the other forms of taxation. This means that the growing state expenditures on social and welfare services have been primarily financed by a higher burden of taxes for the working population. In 1953, the proportion of taxes on wages and salary in total taxes was only 10 percent. This ratio increased to close to 30 percent in the mid-1970's. The recent recessionary trend, characterized by large reserve of the unemployed and an increasing number of households under the poverty line, has undermined the ability of the government to continue to collect the same level of taxes from the working population (see Figure 4.12).

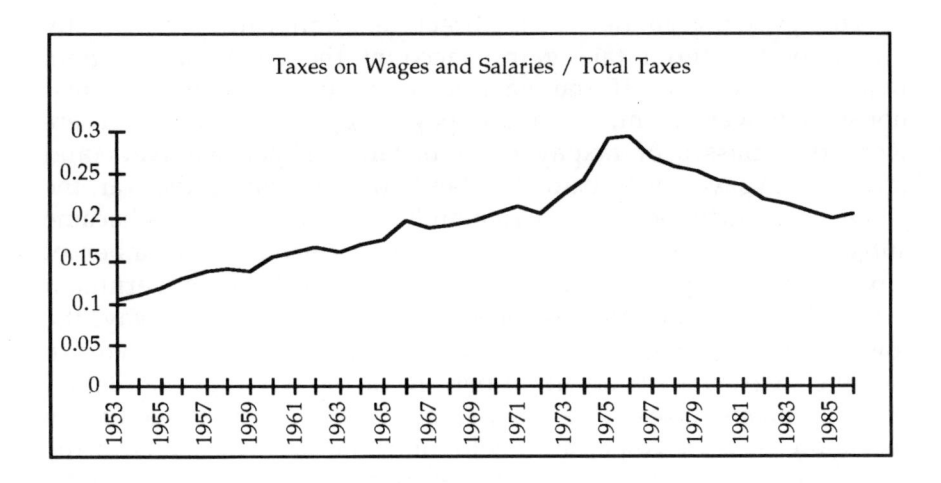

Figure 4.12 The share of taxes on wages and salaries in total taxes

As Figure 4.13 shows, the share of social security and payroll taxes in the total taxes has gone through similar changes. The difference is that both the rate of increase of these taxes and their recent rate of decline have been more moderate. This is because the social security tax is regressive; an increase in its rate would not induce the same level of revenue for the government as the increase in the rate of taxation on wages and salaries would.

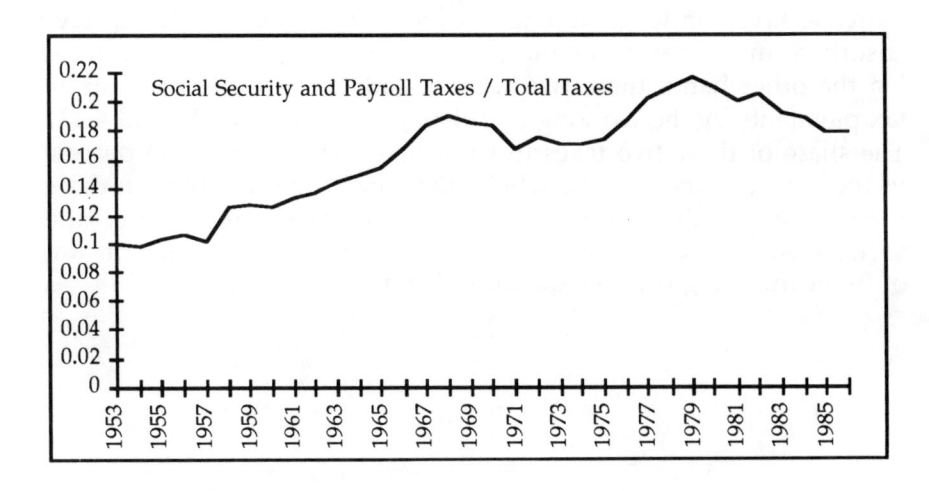

Figure 4.13 The share of social security and payroll taxes in total taxes

The growing tendency of direct taxation can not be fully understood without taking into account the effect of inflation. Before World War II the vast majority of the working class households were exempt from any payment of income taxes. There were two classes of taxpayers in Britain: super-taxpayers and ordinary taxpayers who paid at a standard rate. During the war, the government increased the tax rate and many more incomes became subject to income tax. In this process an increasing number of workers had to pay taxes. After the war, the Labor government reduced the tax rate on both profits and wages. In this way, the lower income groups were mostly exempted from tax payment. By the early 1950's about 30 percent of the working population paid no income taxes. The increasing rate of inflation moved more and more lower income households into the tax net. Thus in the early 1960's, about 90 percent of the working people had to pay some taxes. The rapid inflation of the 1960's and 1970's pushed almost the whole working population into the tax net. As a result of this process, a large proportion of the workers were moved into higher tax brackets and paid income taxes at higher rates. Inflation was therefore a means serving the government to finance the growing costs of the social and welfare programs. Workers were forced to pay increasingly a higher proportion of the costs associated with the provision of social services (see Figure 4.14).

The other noticeable trend is the increasing ratio of income taxes paid by workers over labor income. As Figures 4.13 and 4.15 indicate, taxes on wage and salaries and social security taxes have absorbed an increasing amount of the workers' income over time. On the other hand, these two taxes together constitute the bulk of tax payments by the working population (see Figures 4.16 and 4.17). The share of these two taxes in labor taxes has exceeded 95 percent in the recent years. On the whole, the conclusion that we can draw from these parallel trends is that taxes on wages and salaries and social security taxes have become more and more the major means of financing the growing expenditures on social programs.

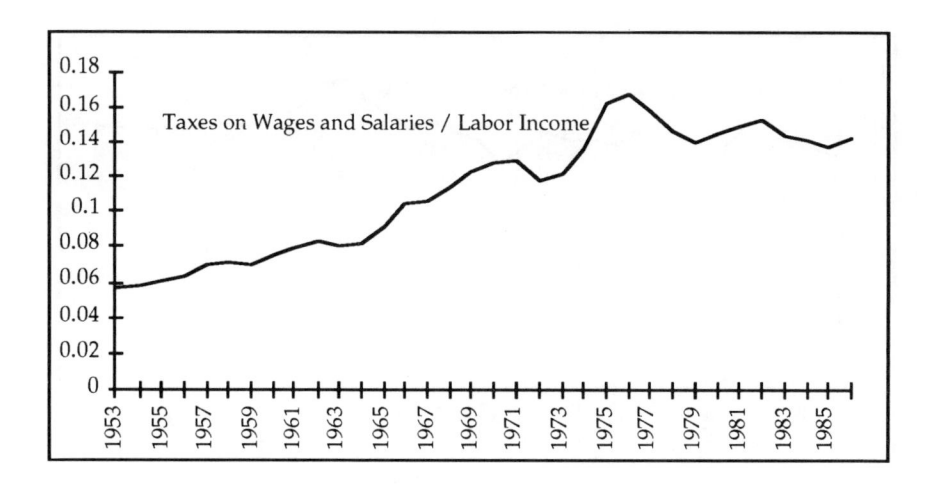

Figure 4.14 The share of taxes on wages and salaries in labor income

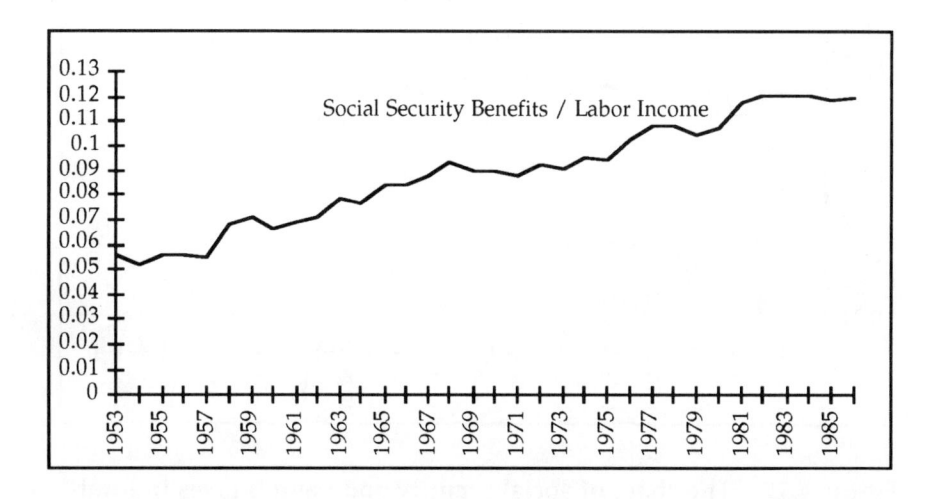

Figure 4.15 The share of social security benefits in labor income

103

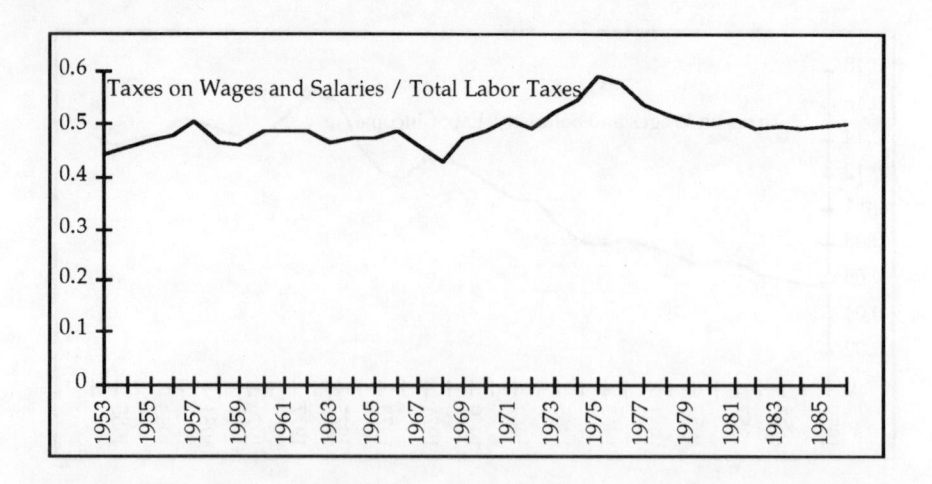

Figure 4.16 The share of taxes on wages and salaries in total labor taxes

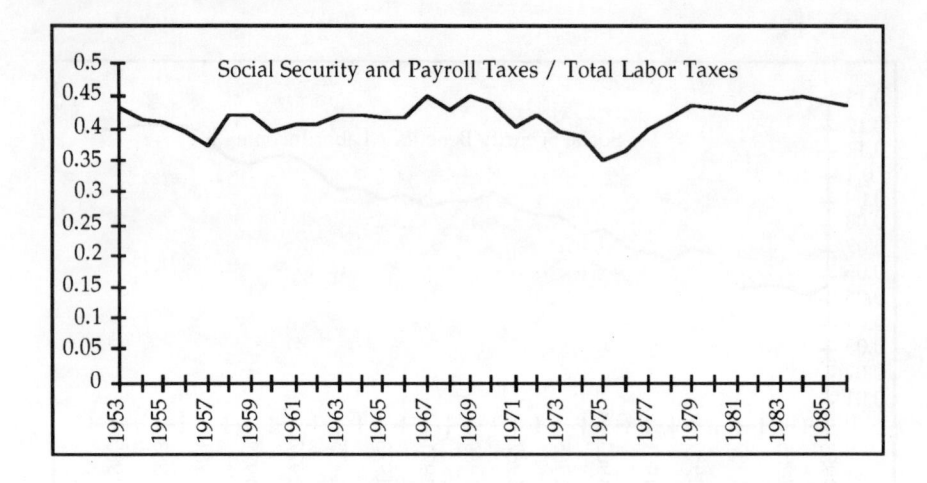

Figure 4.17 The share of social security and payroll taxes in total taxes

The second group consists of Other Individual Income Taxes, Taxes on Immovable Property Paid by Households and Other Taxes which are paid by all households. The share of labor in these is assumed to be proportional to the share of total labor income in personal income. Other taxes are for the most part charges for government services at a market or subsidized prices. The share of this item in total taxes has not been significant and has declined in recent years (see Figure 4.18). The tax on immovable property has slightly increased over time, but its share in total taxes is still insignificant (see Figure 4.19).

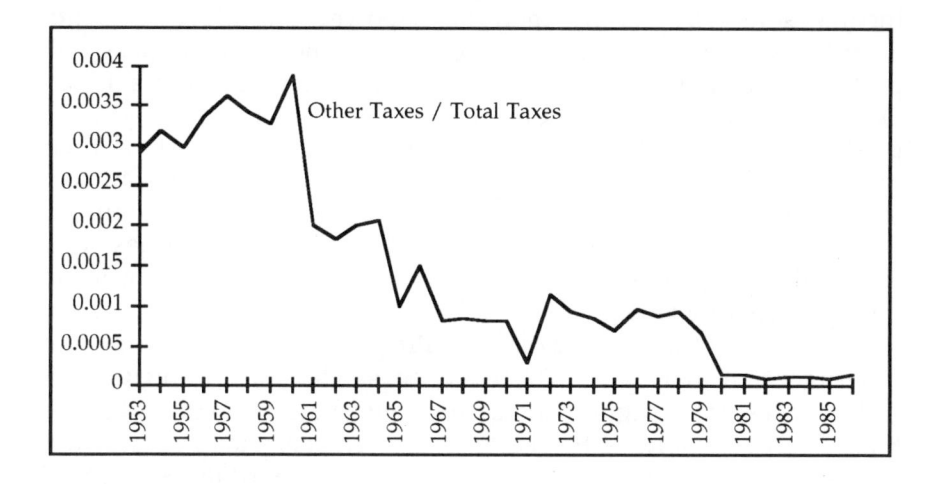

Figure 4.18 The share of other taxes in total taxes

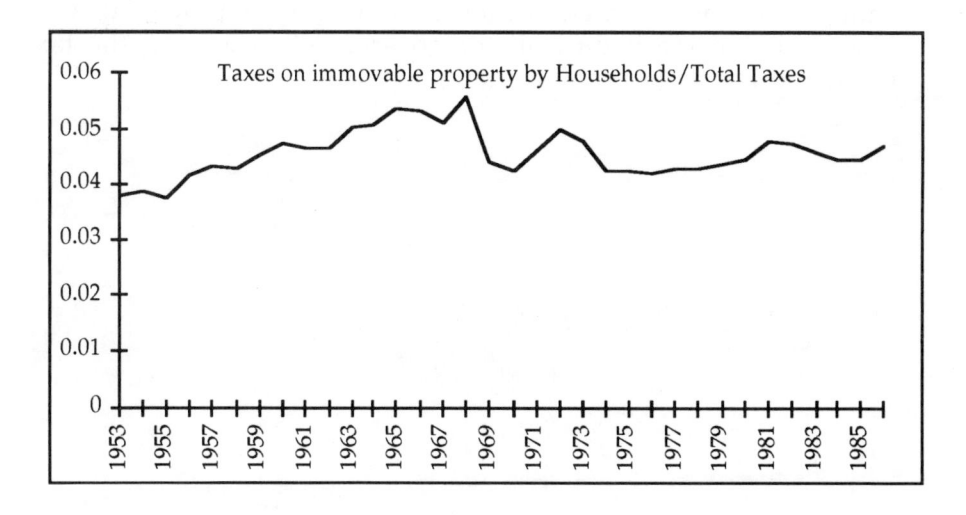

Figure 4.19 The share of taxes on immovable property by households in total taxes

105

The third group includes those taxes which are assumed not to be directly paid by workers. All taxes paid by business belong to this group.

No estate and gift taxes are assumed for working people and hence their share in the tax on these items is considered to be zero. The same is true for corporate income. The workers are also assumed to own no stocks and shares. They are assumed to receive income solely by selling their labor-power. While this is not completely true, other incomes received by the working class will probably not constitute a significant fraction of wages and salaries. On the other hand, all taxes on wages and salaries are assumed to be paid by workers. Capitalists may receive a small part of their income in the form of salaries. This method should not lead to a considerable underestimation taxes paid by workers. Furthermore, the benefits received from non-allocated goods and subsidies were assumed to be proportional to the fraction of wages and salaries in total personal income.

The proportion of Taxes on Property, Gift, Wealth, and Inheritance in total taxes has remained stable. Profit and Capital Gains Taxes have slightly increased their share in total taxes (see Figure 4.21). In spite of the Thatcher government's tax policy which has been more favorable to the business, the share of taxes on profit in total taxes has increased in recent years. This is because, on the one hand, the share of profit in the national income has increased and, on the other hand, the expansion of unemployment and poverty has made it difficult for government to expand the tax revenue collected from the working population.

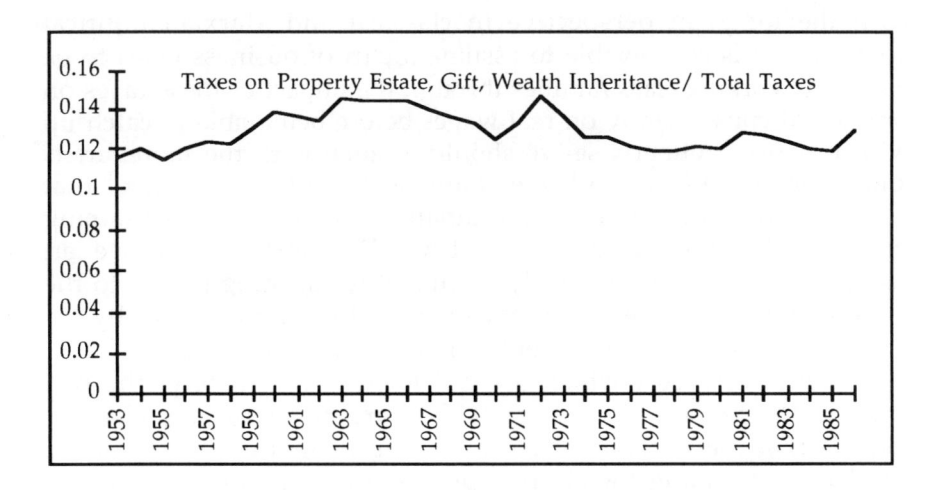

Figure 4.20 The share of taxes on property estate, gift, wealth inheritance in total taxes

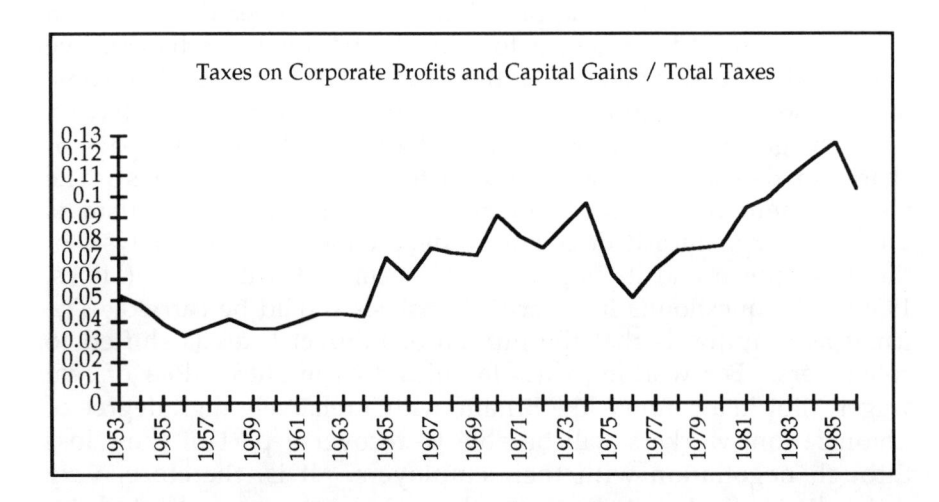

Figure 4.21 The share of taxes on corporate profits and capital gains in total taxes

To measure the influence of indirect business taxes on the working population, we need to discuss two alternative approaches. The first approach is based on the assumption that these taxes are a deduction from surplus value (or profit). This method is consistent with the long-run perspective in classical and Marxian political economy. It is conceivable to assume a part of business taxes to be borne by working class families through the impact of these taxes on prices and consequently on real wages before being able to catch up with inflation. Otherwise we should assume with the monetarists and more specifically with the "Rational Expectations" school that workers' exact predictions of the inflation rate and their bargaining power will eliminate this possibility. This approach, however, seems to attribute an extremely harmonious adjusting power to the market forces. But the measurement of the loss of real wages by the workers due to the incidence of business taxes is not easy.

For indirect taxes which are not levied immediately, the one who has to pay proceeds to shift the burden somewhere else. It follows that the analysis of the operation of indirect taxes can be studied by pursuing the shifting process to the point of incidence. In the analysis of shifting we need to discover a real taxpayer other than the party who is formally paying to the revenue authorities. The available literature does not lead to a careful analysis of the process. It seems that the difference in the classification of taxes into direct/indirect is in their application. We face other difficulties in using burden and incidence for the discussion of redistributive impact which is our concern in this study. For instance, an income tax can not be shifted; but in the case of an indirect tax we have a party the government wants to tax and a party who actually pays or shares in the payment of the tax to the revenue authorities. The measurement of the tax incidence in the shifting mechanism is unsatisfactory, since it does not go deep enough in the analysis of this mechanism and its impact on the income distribution. (Hicks, 1956). The question is how far this analysis should be carried. The usual assumption is that the burden of indirect taxes is shifted to consumers. For working class families, this implies a loss of real wages. But in a country like Britain, with a relatively high degree of unionization, workers will be able to recover a part of their loss through negotiation with their employers. It is, therefore, very difficult to find out how much real wages are affected by expenditures taxes.

The second approach is based on the assumption that indirect taxes are fully reflected in final prices and are thus allocated in accordance with household expenditures on various items (OECD, 1987: 206). This is a standard incidence assumption used in various redistributive studies for the United States and the United Kingdom (Musgrave etal., 1974, Pechman and Oknur 1974, Nicholson 1972, and Stephenson 1976). General sales taxes are assumed to be borne by consumers in proportion to their total expenditures based on the assumption that these taxes do not change relative prices and consumption patterns. The initial effect of excise taxes is different, since they do change relative prices. But even in this case in which relative factor and product prices are changed, there will be no change in relative real income if all households are deriving their incomes from the same sources and in the same proportion, and if they have the same consumption patterns. And, in fact, "there is little reason to believe that there is a disproportionate consumption of labor-intensive products and services at one end of the income scale or of capital-intensive products and services at the other end" (Pechman and Oknur.1974: 28). The conclusion derived from this analysis is that the burden of every tax in this category will be proportional to income.

In this book we use two incidence assumptions for measuring the impact of indirect business taxes on the working population. The first assumption is that these taxes are a deduction from surplus value and involve no direct burden for the working population. The above analysis shows that this method may result in an underestimation of the tax burden of the working population and an overestimation of the amount of the net social wage. The results of our study based on this assumption are presented in the following Chapter.

The second incidence assumption is that the burden of indirect business taxes is shifted to households, since they are consumers of the products on which sales, excise taxes, duties, etc., are imposed. The higher prices of products lead to a loss of real wage by workers. The share of the working population in these taxes will be proportional to the share of total wages in personal income or what we have called the "labor share". This assumption is in line with the incidence assumption used in redistributive studies analyzed in the previous section.

One may suggest that this method may lead to the underestimation of the taxes paid by working class families who spend a higher proportion of their income on consumption goods than high income families. This is of course true, since it is well established that expenditure taxes are, in general, regressive. But on the whole, this method should result in the overestimation of the taxes paid by the working population and the underestimation of the amount of the net social wage. This is because this mechanism of analysis is not carried far enough to examine the entire incidence of this form of taxation. It is true that workers will initially suffer a loss of real wages due to higher prices of consumption goods caused by the imposition of higher general sales and excise taxes on these goods. But it is reasonable to assume that a part or the whole amount of this loss in real wages will be compensated for by the success of workers (particularly unions) to negotiate higher nominal wages to cover for higher prices of consumption goods. The results of our research based on this second incidence assumption is presented in Appendix IV. These two incidence assumptions will lead to the estimation of an upper limit and a lower limit for the real value of the net social wage. Appendixes V and VI will include the adjustments for the self-employed and the top managers.

The share of indirect business taxes in total taxes has moderately declined up to 1975 (see Figure 4.22). This is consistent with the general trend in other advanced capitalist societies in which personal income taxes and social security taxes have grown, while expenditure, and corporate taxes have either stagnated or declined (see Gough, 1979: 96). The recession led the government to increase the rate of taxation on goods and services to compensate for its lost revenue in other areas. This policy started under the last Labor government and was continued with increased intensity under the Thatcher administration. In its first budget, the new Conservative government reduced the standard rate of the income tax from 33 to 30 percent and the corporate tax rate from 83 to 60 percent. In return the government opted for an increase in VAT (Value Added Tax) from 8 to 15 percent and an increase in the petrol tax of 10 percent per gallon. This policy had a distributive role. The increase in indirect taxes, which are considered to be more regressive, implied a greater share of the burden had to be borne by the working population (see Croin and Radtke, 1987: 289).

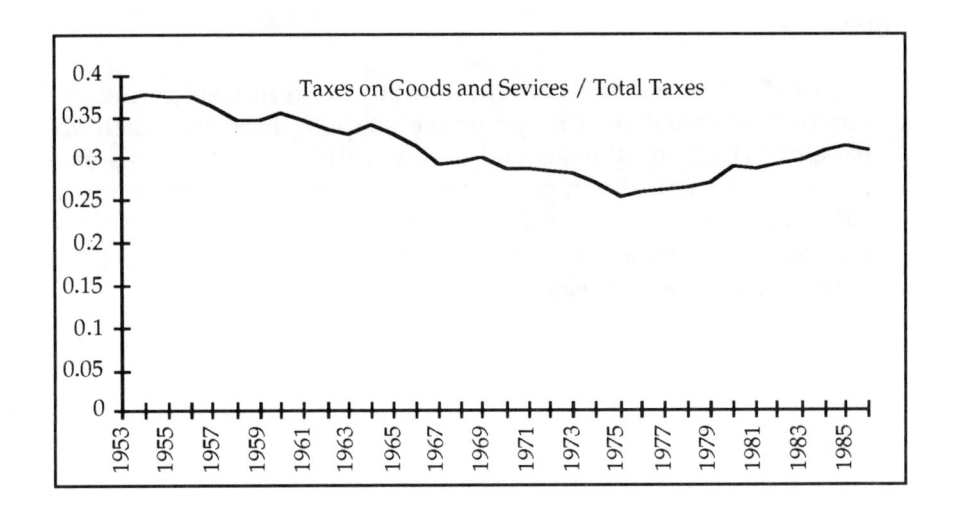

Figure 4.22 The share of taxes on goods and services in total taxes

To estimate the tax equivalent for the self-employed, we must first measure their wage equivalent. We divide the income of the self-employed into two components: a wage equivalent and a profit equivalent. In order to measure their wage equivalent, we multiply the number of the self-employed by the average annual wage of male workers for each year. We have intentionally chosen the average wage of male workers because the wage rate for female workers is consistently lower due to labor market segmentation. This wage equivalence is then multiplied by effective labor tax rate to derive the income tax equivalent for the self-employed. The effective labor tax rate is measured by dividing taxes on wages and salaries by total wages. To calculate the share of workers and the self-employed for the second group of taxes, we apply the same method used for the expenditure side. In other words, we multiply the total value of these taxes by the adjusted labor share in which the wage equivalent of the self-employed is taken into account.

In the following Chapter, the results of this study for the period 1953-1986 are presented. The net transfer or net social wage is the difference between total social benefits received by workers and total taxes paid by them.

Notes

1. We have discussed this concept in more detail in chapter one.
2. For further detail on this point see chapter three in which we have criticized the Bowles and Gintis method counting this as a tax on profit paid by capital. In studies by Nicholson prior to 1969, this item is counted as a direct tax by labor. In the subsequent studies, this item is considered as an indirect tax contributing to an increase in market prices.

5 The results and the concluding analysis

The following conclusion may be drawn from the empirical findings of this research. The share of gross social consumption in the total consumption of the workers has increased (see Figure 5.3), where is indicative of the rising role of the state in the reproduction of the labor power. In Figure 5.3 both the benefits received by the working population and taxes paid by them as a proportion of their overall income for the period of our study, 1953-1986, are presented. Assuming that workers' income is in most part spent on consumption, this ratio can be used as a good indicator to show the relative importance of the publicly provided or publicly financed consumption of workers and their families relative to their private or market consumption. This ratio has increased from 21 percent in 1953 to 31 percent in 1986. This trend represents a relatively modest tendency toward an increased collectivization of consumption and does not reflect any substantial transformation in the economic structure of British society. Workers should still primarily depend on their wage income and their ability to sell their labor services in the market in order to make their subsistence.

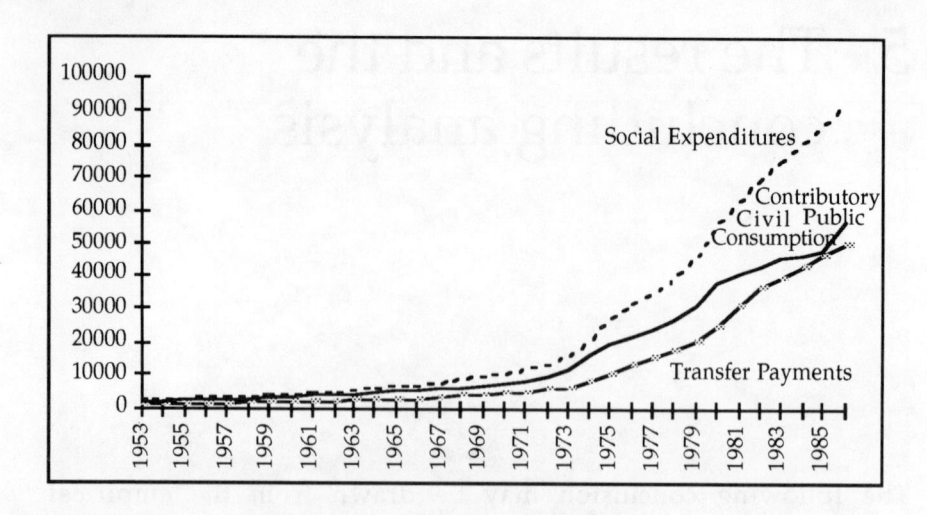

Figure 5.1 Transfer payments, social expenditures, and civil public consumption

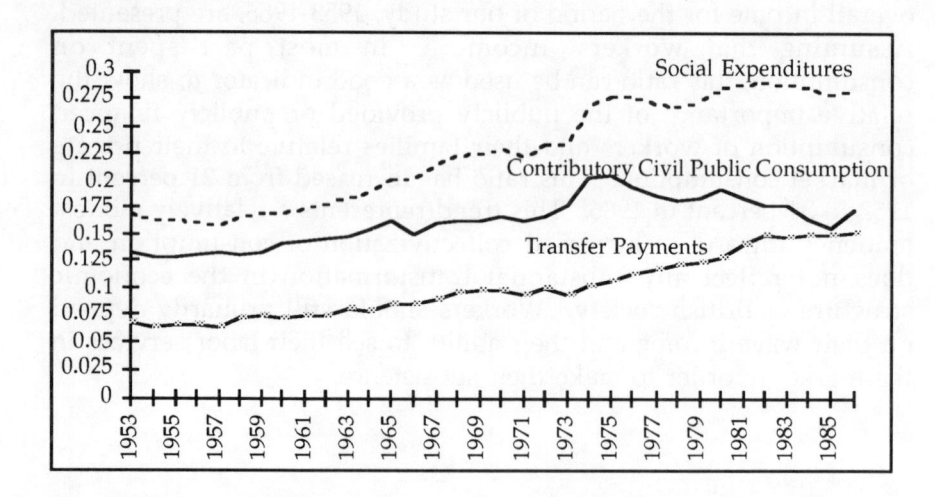

Figure 5.2 Transfer payments, social expenditures, and civil public consumption as percentage of GNP

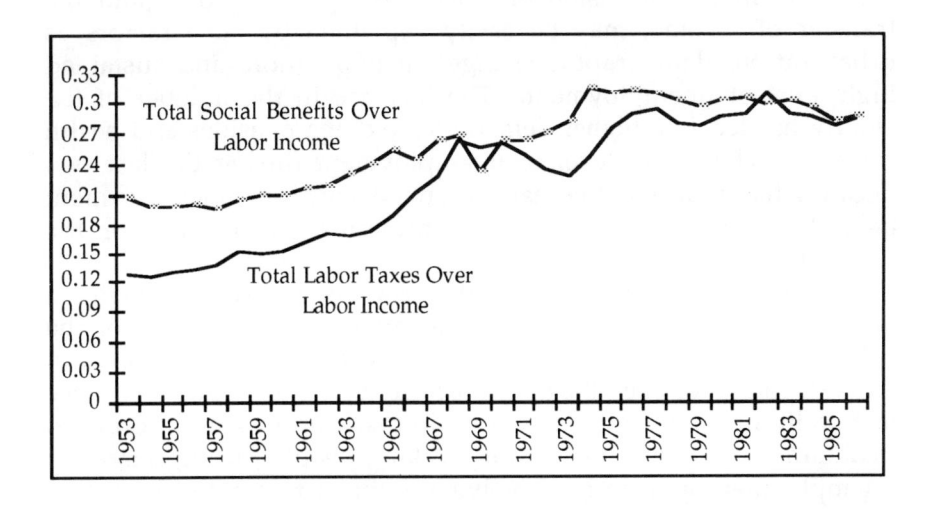

Figure 5.3 Total labor taxes over labor income and total labor social benefits over labor income

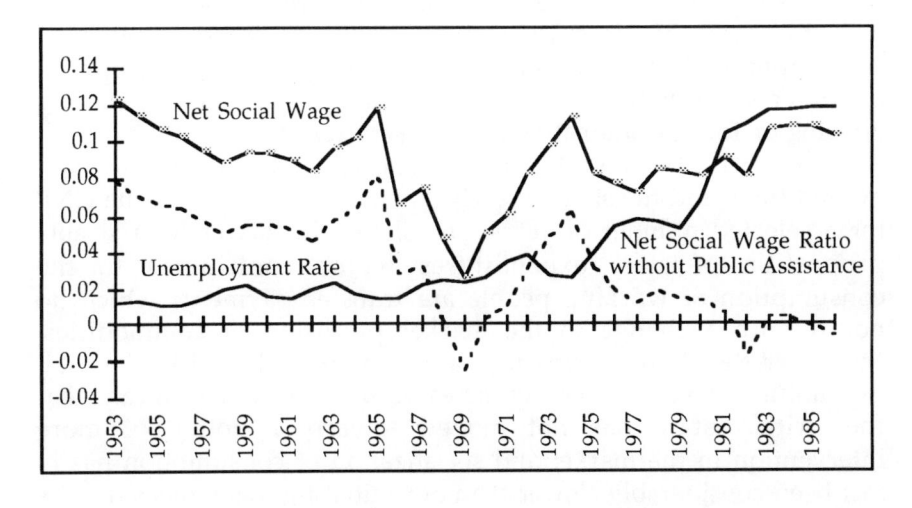

Figure 5.4 Net social wage ratio adjusted for self employed and unemployment rate

Such a gradual and moderate increase in the importance of the state role in the provision of "social" or "public goods" and the transfer of income, may be easily explained by such factors as urbanization, demographic changes in population, and sustained high level of unemployment. The increase in the number of the elderly has led to a higher demand for old age pensions and health services. The rising level of unemployment during the last two decades has required the state to spend more on unemployment benefits in order to guarantee a minimum subsistence for the unemployed.

On the other hand, the rise in the proportion of social benefits in labor income cannot entirely be interpreted as a reflection of the collectivization tendency. The first group of state expenditures in our categorization, i.e., the social security benefits, public assistance and welfare, comprise the subsidies in cash and in kind in order to maintain a minimum income for working people during phases of unemployment and do not involve any direct transfer of resources from the market sector to the public sector. The cash payments or benefits in kind received by workers are still directed to purchase market-produced commodities and do not lead to a modification in the market provision of goods. It may therefore be inappropriate to call this type of state-financed purchase of goods, collective consumption. The expenditures of the second and third groups, on the other hand, may involve state intervention in markets, such as housing or for educational and health services etc.

Table 5.1 presents the more detailed composition of state expenditures and the share of each expenditure category in the GNP for a selected number of years. As shown in this table, a sizable proportion of state expenditures which contributes to the consumption of working people are transfer payments which do not require a change in the market provision of commodities. Moreover the share of transfer payments in GNP and in the total expenditures has considerably increased over time. This means that the British state has not moved toward a policy of more intervention in the market and socialization of consumption has in fact been considerably slower than our initial figures indicated. The share of housing, transportation, communication, and public utilities in the gross national product has remained stable over time. On the other hand, relative increase in expenditure on education and health does not necessarily represent any substantial increase in the commitment of the state to the improvement of these services or any considerable shift of resources from market to state. From the very beginning of this period in the 1950's, the role of the state in the provision of education and health services has been substantial. The increase in expenditures for these items should not be interpreted as any change in the role of the state. To the extent that this relative increase may reflect any improvement in the quality of these services (particularly up to 1975), this might have happened even if they were provided by the private sector. One would expect that with the increase in productivity and rise in the standards of living, the standard of these service to be upgraded.

The advancement of technology could have also induced higher expenditures on both items. More sophisticated technology requires a greater and better educated labor force. To the degree that this trend leads to the employment of more complex technology in the medical profession, this results in a higher cost for medical services. A part of the increase in these social expenses has been caused by demographic changes: the rise in the number of those under fifteen, from 11.4 million in 1951 to 13.4 million in 1971, which has raised the budget of education, and the increase in the population of the elderly from 6.9 million in 1951 to 9.1 million 1971. Since therefore heavy users of health services, this has led to the rise in health expenses. The higher cost of inflation in the public sector is another factor explaining the relative rise in educational and health expenses. This is because public goods and services and particularly services such as education and health, which are so dependent on human contribution, are subject to lower productivity gains (compared to the industrial production sector). This means that rising nominal expenditures are required just to maintain the same coverage and quality of services.

Table 5.1
Public expenditures trends

Year	1953	% of GNP	1960	% of GNP	1965	% of GNP	1970	% of GNP	1975	% of GNP	1980	% of GNP	1986	% of GNP
Group I														
Social Security Benefits	528	3.49	996	4.36	1783	5.63	2731	6.19	6432	6.75	14689	7.59	25131	7.68
Public Assistance and Welfare	478	3.16	635	2.78	857	2.71	1618	3.67	3855	4.05	10162	5.25	25064	7.66
Transfer Payments	1006	6.66	1631	7.13	2640	8.34	4349	9.86	10287	10.80	24851	12.85	50195	15.34
Group II														
Housing	569	3.77	490	2.14	957	3.02	1319	2.99	4459	4.68	6171	3.19	4195	1.28
Education	457	3.02	890	3.89	1480	4.67	2423	5.49	6453	6.77	12753	6.59	19521	5.96
Health	529	3.50	879	3.84	1303	4.11	2031	4.60	5272	5.54	11629	6.01	19446	5.94
Social Expenditures	2561	16.95	3890	17.01	6380	20.15	10122	22.94	26471	27.79	55404	28.64	93357	28.52
Group III														
Public Utilities, Recreation	142	0.94	241	1.05	400	1.26	612	1.39	1051	1.10	3687	1.91	10183	3.11
Transport, Communication, Public Roads, and Lighting	298	1.97	739	3.23	1025	3.24	983	2.23	2434	2.56	3409	1.76	3681	1.12
(Contributory) Civil Public Consumption	1995	8.72	3239	14.16	5165	16.31	7368	16.70	19669	20.65	37649	19.46	57026	17.42
Gross National Product	15110		22870		31667		44128		95248		193450		327300	

Note: 'Transfer Payments' is the sum of categories in group I. 'Social Expenditures' is the sum of group I and group II. 'Contributory Civil Public Consumption' is defined as those items in Civil Public Consumption contributing to the benefit of the working population. It is the sum of all categories in group II and III.

Hence, while the expansion of the state sector in the post-War II period has led to an increase in the relative importance of collective or social consumption, it has not been as dramatic as might have appeared by looking at the more aggregate numbers. The findings of this research may also be used to evaluate the validity of the views of those who trace the root of the current crisis to the over expansion of public expenditures and particularly the explosive growth of welfare and social programs.

One such argument has been put forward by neoconservatives who blame exaggerated and unrestricted welfare state development in response to the "revolution of rising expectations" which has exceeded the fiscal capacity of the state. In this view, the behavior of individuals in the world of democratic and competitive politics is considered to be virtually similar to behavior in the market economy. It is argued that the competition of parties and politicians in this political market to win elections, encourages excessive expectations by the voters which leads to the overload of government. Hence, the overload occurs because the fulfillment of this constantly growing burden of expectations goes beyond the capacity of the government and the resources available.

There are certain structural similarities between the neoconservative theory of "ungovernability" of the state and the views of some radicals with respect to internal contradictions of state activities. O'Connor (1973), for example, refers to the "fiscal crisis of the state" that will eventually be transformed into a "legitimating crisis" of the capitalist parliamentary democracy. For him, the fiscal crisis is the product of the contradiction between the two central functions of the state, i.e., the accumulation and the legitimating functions. There are the rising costs to fulfill its legitimating function and the constraint in the resources available to the state, because the revenue of the state to finance these rising expenditures is dependent on capital accumulation which is controlled by the private sector. To explain the rising expenditures of the state associated with the legitimating aspect, he refers to the pressure of interest groups and the rising expectations of the participants in the political market. He argues that the state is expected to take responsibility for many things while it has no control over production resources which are mainly in private hands. His analysis of the rising expectation has a striking similarity to the neoconservative line of argument. He writes: "Every economic and social class and group wants government to spend more and more money on more and more things. But no one wants to pay new taxes or higher rates on old taxes. Indeed, nearly everyone wants lower taxes, and many groups have agitated successfully for tax relief" (O'Connor 1973: 1).

Government expenditures have, in fact, increased substantially in Britain during the post-War II period. The proportion of public expenditures in GNP has increased from about 30 percent in 1950 up to close to 50 percent in recent years. But a large part of this increase may be explained by factors, such as economic growth, demographic changes, and the rising relative costs of public services (as compared with market-produced commodities). The overall rise in public expenditures by itself does not tell us much about the dynamics unleashed by political pressures and rising expectations or increasing costs involved in the legitimating function of the state in a system of liberal democracy. To analyze such a process, we need to look at the components of state expenditures and find out what type of expenditures have been the driving force in public expenditures growth.

If the state expenditures development is less determined by economic growth and other structural factors and is instead primarily determined by political and ideological factors, then the main deriving forces of these expenditures should have been the social transfer payments and other components of the social expenditures, such as health, housing and education. It is reasonable to expect that the articulated demands of the electorate and pressure groups should be primarily directed toward social security and the provision of social services rather than other expenditures, such as defense, infrastructure, and communications, which may not produce any direct and visible benefits to the electorate. This is also the case for those views in which the class struggle is conceived to be the main driving force of rising state activities as the disproportionate growth of social expenditures may be explained by the growing political power of the working class who have first struggled for social security and later for income redistribution. This line of analysis is particularly supported by Bowles and Gintis (1982) who argue that the success of workers in their struggles for social benefits has resulted in the rise of a net redistributive gain for them or what they call "citizen wage."

Indeed, the evidence derived from the trend of public expenditures in the United Kingdom seems to be supporting such expectations. The value of social expenditures in the U.K. has risen faster than public expenditures as a whole. As Table 5.1 shows, social expenditures have increased from close to 17 percent of GNP in 1953 to close to 30 percent in 1980. This is an increase of nearly twice which is considerably higher than the growth of public expenditures as a whole. But, as we discussed before, the relative rise in education and health expenses has largely been caused by factors such as the overall rate of economic growth, demographic changes, and the higher cost of inflation due to lower productivity increase in these services which are highly labor intensive. The trend of the recent decade also shows that the rise in these expenditures is highly conditioned by the overall performance of the economy. The share of educational expenses in the gross national product has declined after 1975. This ratio for health services moderately increased from 1975 to 1980 and declined in the later period. This is at the same time when, as the current debate in the U.S. and in Britain reveals, the costs of medical services have been increasing considerably making it difficult for the state to maintain even the same level of services without substantial increases in the budget. In the post-1975 period even the ratio of social security benefits over GNP has not increased substantially, while in the same period the rising rate of unemployment has required the state to grant more benefits to workers who have not been able to find employment. The expenditures on housing have vastly fluctuated (see tables 5.2 and 5.3) and in recent years have absorbed less resources than they did in the 1950's.

Table 5.2
Periodization of public expenditures programs

Period	Average Annual Percentage Rate of Increase							Adjusted for Inflation				
	1953-57	1957-64	1964-70	1970-74	1974-79	1979-86	1953-57	1957-64	1964-70	1970-74	1974-79	1979-86
(1) Defense and External Relations	-1.18	4.00	3.53	14.16	17.37	9.58	-4.82	1.37	-1.19	3.18	1.82	1.47
(2) Trade, Industry, Agriculture, and Employment Services	8.67	5.70	8.82	9.84	13.44	1.53	5.03	3.05	4.10	-1.13	-2.11	-6.58
(3) Administration Expenses and Others	5.56	0.00	12.22	21.76	16.66	7.94	1.92	1.99	7.50	10.78	1.11	-0.17
(4) Police, Prison, and Fire	0.28	6.68	10.81	17.68	19.14	12.58	-3.36	4.02	6.09	6.71	3.59	4.47
(5) Social Security Benefits	7.46	11.44	10.47	16.09	19.47	11.04	3.82	8.79	5.75	5.12	3.92	2.93
(6) Public Assistance and Welfare	3.33	5.67	12.41	15.07	25.04	16.37	-0.31	3.02	7.69	4.10	9.49	8.26
(7) Housing	-4.67	8.16	8.38	33.65	4.95	-3.44	-8.31	5.50	3.66	22.68	-10.60	-11.55
(8) Education	11.72	9.38	10.46	16.52	18.21	9.55	8.08	6.73	5.74	5.55	2.66	1.43
(9) Health	7.21	7.45	9.85	18.02	18.18	11.49	3.57	4.79	5.13	7.04	2.63	3.38
(10) Public Utilities, Recreation	7.69	9.74	8.95	10.34	27.27	18.91	4.05	7.08	4.23	-0.64	11.72	10.80
(11) Transport, Communication, Public Roads, and Lighting	14.38	8.83	1.07	19.37	10.18	1.84	10.74	6.17	-3.65	8.40	-5.37	-6.28
(12) Interest, Capital Consumption and Others	0.00	5.19	3.01	26.98	19.73	9.67	0.00	2.53	-1.71	16.00	4.18	1.55
(13) Total Expenditure	0.054	0.062	0.119	0.113	0.171	0.124	0.018	0.035	0.072	0.003	0.015	0.043

A Chronology of Government
- 1953-1957: Conservative Government
- 1957-1964: Conservative Government
- 1964-1974: Labor Government
- 1970-1974: Conservative Government
- 1974-1979: Labor Government
- 1979-1986: Thatcherite Conservative Government

Table 5.3
Post-War cycles (economy and social expenditures)

Cycle	I		II		III		IV		V		VI	
Period	1953-57	Adjusted for Inf.	1957-64	Adjusted for Inf.	1964-70	Adjusted for Inf.	1970-74	Adjusted for Inf.	1974-79	Adjusted for Inf.	1979-86	Adjusted for Inf.
Duration	4 years		7 years		6 years		4 years		5 years		7 years	
Group I												
Social Security Benefits	7.50	3.80	11.40	8.80	10.50	5.70	16.10	5.10	19.50	3.90	11.00	2.60
Public Assistance and Welfare	3.30	-0.30	5.70	3.00	12.40	7.70	15.10	4.10	25.00	9.50	16.40	8.30
Transfer Payments	5.50	1.90	9.10	6.50	11.20	6.40	15.70	4.70	21.60	6.10	13.50	5.30
Group II												
Housing	-4.70	-8.30	8.20	5.50	8.40	3.70	33.70	22.70	4.90	-10.60	-3.40	-11.60
Education	11.70	8.10	9.40	6.70	10.50	5.70	16.50	5.50	18.20	2.70	9.50	1.40
Health	7.20	3.60	7.50	4.80	9.80	5.10	18.00	7.00	18.20	2.60	11.50	3.40
Social Expenditures	5.10	1.50	8.70	6.00	10.30	5.60	19.20	8.20	17.40	1.80	10.80	2.70
Group III												
Public Utilities, Recreation	7.70	4.10	9.70	7.10	8.90	4.20	10.30	-0.60	27.30	11.70	18.90	10.80
Transport, Communication, Public Roads, and Lighting	14.40	10.70	8.80	6.20	1.10	-3.60	19.40	8.40	10.20	-5.40	1.80	-6.30
(Contributory) Civil Public Consumption	6.70	3.00	8.60	5.90	8.20	3.50	20.50	9.50	14.90	-0.70	12.00	3.89
Net Social Wage	-0.70	-4.34	7.98	5.32	-33.29	-38.01	136.01	125.03	-10.62	-26.17	-30.51	-38.63
Unemployment Rate	1.25		2.30		2.40		3.80		5.80		11.50	
Inflation: % Average Annual Rise in Price Index	3.60		2.70		4.70		11.00		15.50		8.10	
Budget Deficit	17.90	14.20	10.20	7.60	-25.40	-30.10	80.20	69.30	11.20	-4.40	-0.80	-8.90
Gross National Product	6.76	3.11	6.05	3.39	6.88	2.16	14.59	3.61	19.50	1.52	10.06	1.95

Note: All measurements are the percent average annual rise in that category except for unemployment. 'Transfer Payment' is the sum of categories in Group I. 'Social Expenditures' is the sum of Group I and Group II. '(Contributory Civil Public Consumption)' is the sum of categories in Group II and III.

While the rise in social security, health, and educational benefits has been more or less a function of economic growth, public assistance and welfare expenditures have been conversely related to the rate of economic growth and the performance of the economy. Family allowances, supplementary benefits, and other welfare expenses constituted a small proportion of GNP in the 1960's when the economy was booming and both rates of unemployment and inflation were considerably less. It increased to a significant degree in late the 1970's and 1980's, in a period of mounting unemployment and rising inflation which made it difficult for the wages of those who were working at the lower tier jobs to catch up with rising prices. The expansion of low paying jobs in the retail and services sectors and the rising number of single parent families forced a large number of families into poverty. In any case, the increase in public assistance does not represent any extension of entitlements as the model of rising expectations or the model of class struggle induced rise in social rights may suggest.

This is not to suggest that the political considerations of the type put forward by the political competition or class struggle models have not made any contribution to the trend of social expenditures development. But the political effect tends to be swamped by the dictates of the economic constraints. To take into account the influence of ideological differences and the organized strength of the working class, we turn now to the analysis of the party composition of government. The political market model implies that parties behave more or less in similar ways. This is because they all compete in the political market to win the support of the electorate who demand the expansion and improvement of services. The competition of the pressure groups to increase the public provision of services which serves their interest best will also intensify the expansion of public expenditures. These models, as Klein (1976) observes, "treat voters as though they were consumers shopping around for the best buy in the market place" and hence "ignore the role of the party ideology" (p.406).

It is assumed that increased welfare spending is most favored by the working population and particularly by its poorest strata because of their urgent needs for income maintenance programs and their potential gains from those programs aimed at income redistribution. The working population on the whole should be supportive of increased social security benefits, since workers are more susceptible to the insecurity of market fluctuation and the risk of losing their subsistence. Public housing or subsidies for housing are also more critical for the working population and especially the poor.

The benefits of other items of social expenditures, health and education, are shared by different classes. But if we take the tax considerations into account, we should expect the working population to be more supportive of increased health services, while the middle and upper classes are more resistant to the excessive expansion of those services, since they may have the means to purchase these services from the private sector. The case of education differs to some extent because the educational facilities of the school provide services to the local residents and are also financed by taxes paid by them. Hence, those localities with a higher proportion of larger income families would be more supportive of increased spending on schooling than the poor areas.

The benefits of agricultural and industrial subsidies are directly enjoyed by farmers and business. The benefits of some other categories, such as transportation, communication, utilities, etc., are received by business and households as a whole. It is generally assumed that such benefits are not as visible to the electorate as social expenditures and it is very difficult for voters to assign a particular benefit to themselves from these expenditures (Klein 1976: 405).

The political articulation and aggregation of these interests are mainly structured by the level of organizational power of each class or group and by the existing party system. One may expect that the Labor Party would stand for those programs advancing the interests of the working population and social justice. It may be further expected for the Labor Party would adopt a more interventionist policy leading to the overall increase in public expenditures. Conversely, the Conservative Party is expected to oppose the welfare state development and also increased expenditures beyond the classic functions of the state in a capitalist economy. To the extent that public expenditure is allowed by conservatives, it is expected that it should be directed at the expansion of defense and those programs whose benefits are received by business and the middle and upper classes.

If we compare the era of Conservative rule of 1953-1964 with the Labor Government of 1964-1970, this pattern of expectations may be found to be consistent. To take the whole period from 1953 to 1964 we can find that public expenditures as a whole and social expenditures in particular grew at a lower rate than 1964-1970 when the Labor Party was holding office. Public expenditures were increasing at an annual rate of 2.75 percent. This rate reached 4.18

percent during the period 1964-1970 under the Labor Government. In the period 1953-1964, social security benefits, health, public assistance and welfare, and housing increased at the annual rates of 4.75, 3.99, 0.30, and 0.10 percent. The comparable rates for 1964-1970 were 5.75, 5.13, 7.69, and 3.66 percent.

But to derive such a conclusion is misleading. We should distinguish between two consecutive periods of Conservative Governments in this period. During the first Conservative Government, 1953-1957, the rate of growth of public expenditures and social expenditures was substantially lower (see Table 5.2). As shown in Table 5.2 and 5.3, public assistance and welfare and housing had a negative annual growth in real terms. Transfer payments and social expenditures grew at very modest real rates of 1.90 and 1.50 percent, while these expenditures rose at annual rates of 11.2 and 10.3 percent during the Labor Government of 1964-1970. The only exception was education which increased at a fast rate in the period 1953-1957. This pattern should be explained by stating that the first post-War II Conservative Government was still supporting the old liberal ideological laissez-faire tradition. While it reluctantly accepted the basic structure of the welfare state set up by the Labor as a result of the accord of the war period between the state, capital, and labor, it nevertheless was resistant to the expansion of welfare policies and the adoption of an interventionist policy of the Keynesian type.

The turning point in the post-war history of public expenditures came after Harold Macmillan took office. The Conservative Government of Macmillan adopted a markedly more interventionist policy. A comparison of the total public expenditures and social expenditures between the Macmillan Government, 1957-1964, and the Labor Government of Wilson in 1964-1970, shows that they have generally been comparable. The analysis of the post-Macmillan period, in particular before the rise of Thatcherism, reveals that the difference between the actual social policies (and economic policies) of the governments led by the two parties was not very significant. The convergence occurred because all governments, regardless of party and ideology, accepted the main premises of the welfare state and the use of public expenditures as the means for economic management. In so far as the growth of the welfare state was not perceived to threaten the economic growth and capital accumulation, this relative harmony between the policies of parties could be maintained. There were some minor differences in policies, the most notable of which was the discrepancy between expenditures on public assistance and welfare, and transportation and communication. The Labor Governments tended to pay more attention to public assistance (as compared with the Conservative Governments). This can be explained by both ideological differences and the need of the Labor Party to maintain the support of the lower class. It should be noted that public assistance continued to rise at a slightly lower rate under the Thatcher Government. But this increase was induced by the necessity to maintain a minimum subsistence for the poor, the number of which had increased and their conditions worsened in the recent decade. There is no apparent reason for the difference between spending on transportation and communication.

The convergence was most probably between the actual policies, but the intended policies continued to differ to some degree. An example of this is the plan of the Heath Government for drastic cuts in spending in line with what may be called the "ideological model." But rising unemployment and the widespread strike of workers who fought its restrictive wage policy forced the government to reverse the direction of change (see Table 5.2 and Figure 5.5). Even the intended policy was adopted due to emerging growing difficulties of 1970's, in particular the rising rate of inflation which for the first time in the post-war period rose to a double-digit rate of 11 percent. The austerity program which the Heath Government was forced to give up was later adopted by the Labor Government of 1974-1979. Except for public assistance and welfare spending which were required to rise due to increasing unemployment and poverty, the growth of other social expenditures was seriously halted in this period. As Tables 4.2 and 4.3 show, the rate of growth of both transfer payments and social expenditures declined to an unprecedented level comparable only to the period of the first post-war Conservative Government, 1953-1957.

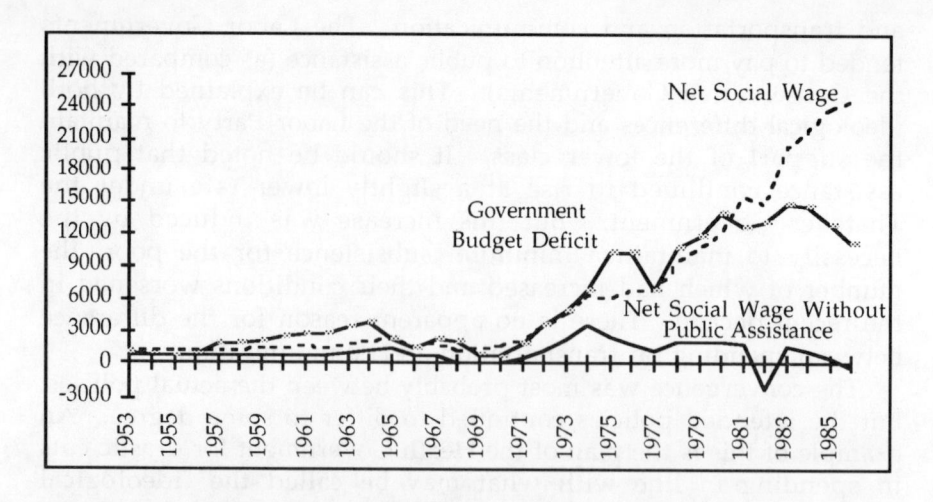

Figure 5.5 Government budget deficit and net social wage (with and without public assistance)

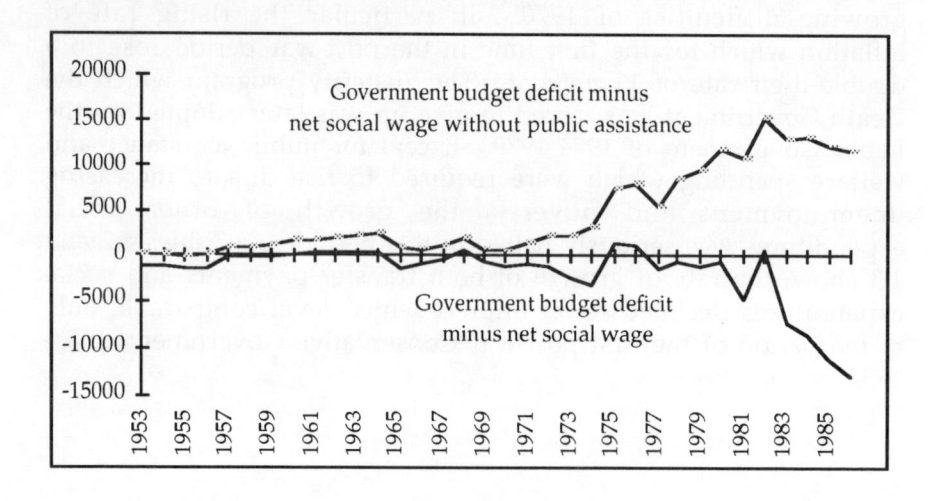

Figure 5.6 Government budget deficit minus net social wage (with and without public assistance)

The actual policy adopted by the Labor Government was a reversal of promises it made throughout its electoral campaign. Within a few months after the party came to office, the promised policy was abandoned and replaced by an austerity program of cutbacks in spending growth and an income policy aimed to control the increase in wages. The highly conservative plan of the Thatcher Government, on the other hand, had to be moderated in actuality, after facing with the economic and political realities. However, there should be no doubt that the rise of Thatcherism, which was itself a product of the economic failures of 1970's and the campaign of business to restrict wage increases, rising welfare spending, the welfare and tax-backlash of the middle and upper classes, in turn led to significant changes in the dominant ideology and the political environment in the society.

As we discussed, the "overload" theory has two aspects: one is growing expectations of the electorate and interest groups and the second aspect is the limitation in the capacity of governments to cope with these excessive expectations. It is this discrepancy between "inflating claims" and the performance capacity of the state which leads to the crisis of ungovernability. This is also true in the case of the "fiscal crisis of the state" theory in which the legitimating requirements (or social expenses) may go beyond the capacity of the state, being itself dependent on private capital for its revenue. It is therefore implied that a widening gap between public expenditures and revenues will evolve over time.

This means that our analysis of social expenditure trends and the validity of the above theories remains incomplete without taking into account the consequences of taxation. The capacity of governments to collect the necessary taxes to finance rising social expenditures may be impaired by the economic constraints of the system. The problem of "overload" or "fiscal crisis" may appear either when tax policies aimed to provide the required social benefits to the working population lead to the shift of the tax burden to capital and in this way impairs the prospects of capital accumulation and dries up the surplus required for future developments of the welfare state, or when governments, unable to increase taxes on workers when their income base is shrinking due to rising unemployment and declining real wages, opt to finance rising social expenditures through an expanding deficit spending which goes out of control.

It is therefore necessary to consider both benefits received by workers and taxes paid by them. We call the net benefit/tax burden of the working population, "net social wage." These findings are presented in Figures 5.3 to 5.6. The results introduced in this Chapter are based on the incidence assumption that indirect business taxes are fully financed by the business sector. It is understood that indirect business taxes play role on real wages. It is, however, suggested that the trend of real wages can be studied separately. The alternative incidence assumption applied in this study is that indirect taxes are fully reflected in prices of products and their burden is shifted to the household sector. The burden of the working population for these taxes will be proportional to the share of total wages in personal income (For further detail on methodology, see Chapter three). The results on the basis of this assumption are presented in Appendix IV.

The analysis of the net social wage trend in the following section is based on the first incidence assumption. In the last section of this Chapter, we will discuss how the application of the second incidence assumption may change the results and their implications for the development of the welfare state in the post-war period.

In Figure 5.3, both benefits received and taxes paid by workers as a percentage of labor income are presented. The increasing weight of social benefits in labor income is indicative of the tendency towards a higher level of collectivization of consumption, but the increasing proportion of taxes shows that the working population has paid for the whole or a large part of its social or publicly supported consumption.

In Figure 5.4 the results of "net social wage ratio" with and without public assistance and unemployment rate are presented. Net social wage ratio is defined as the proportion of the net social wage in workers' income. In the section on "Empirical Methodology," we explained why there are good reasons to use both criteria of the net social wage. The difference between the two is public assistance and welfare expenses (see Table 2a in Appendix I). The comparison of the two concepts of the net social wage will lead to a more illuminating picture regarding the development patterns of the welfare state in the last decade.

Figure 5.5 presents the results of these two concepts of the net social wage alongside the trend of budget deficit over the period of our study. The existence of a net social wage by itself does not provide an adequate basis to argue for any redistribution of income from capital to labor. The excess of social benefits received by workers over their contribution to taxation may also be covered by the budget deficit or borrowing. In a fast growing economy, the government may opt to finance its increasing social expenditures and other categories of public expenditures by deficit spending and borrowing without running into any significant problem. Under these circumstances, it can postpone the repayment of its debt indefinitely. But in a declining economy, rising deficit spending and public debt will adversely affect the overall state of the economy through its intensifying effects on certain key macroeconomic variables, such as the inflation rate and the interest rate. Paradoxically, the government's need for deficit spending and increased borrowing requirements will rise with the slow-down of the economy. Under these conditions, the so-called "overload" or what is characterized by O'Connor as the "fiscal crisis of the state" can result.

In Figure 5.6 the net difference between the budget deficit and the value of the net social wage both with and without public assistance is presented. A positive value indicates that the entire net social wage is covered by the deficit spending of the state. A negative number implies that the amount of the budget deficit has not been adequate to cover the whole net social wage. In the second case, it is probable that the net social wage has been partly covered by the taxes on profit, capital gain, or on non-working population families. Parallel results for the net social wage for the working population and the self-employed are presented in Appendix II in Figures II.1, II.2, II.3, and II.4. In Appendix III, similar results for the adjustment for the top managers are included. In this section, the share of the top managers in benefits and in taxes is deducted from results. The following analysis is based on these results. Since the trend of the net social wage is similar in all these three cases, the same analysis can be applied to all.

The share of workers in the benefits of public expenditures in the United Kingdom, exceeded their share of the tax burden. This net benefit, however, lost its significance over time and more or less disappeared by the mid-1970's (see Figures 5.4 and 5.5). The decline in the net social benefits of workers which had already started under the last Labor Government (1974-1979), continued to decline at an increasing rate under Thatcher's government. The monetarist approach of the government has resulted in high interest rates and rising unemployment. A high rate of unemployment (about 12 percent in 1987) and the fact that many new jobs generated are part-time, temporary or casual jobs, has made heavy demands on the public budget. In spite of this situation, the net benefit of workers has declined and workers have ended up paying even more in taxes than received in benefits. However, the net social benefit, including public assistance, has been rising over the last decade (see Figures 4.2

and 4.3). This is because public assistance and welfare expenses have been increasing on a much faster rate than social security benefits which is itself the result of economic slow-down, persistent unemployment and poverty. The continuing high rate of unemployment means that a large number of workers become gradually separated from the labor force and join the population of the poor. This would increase the demand for welfare and public assistance expenses of the government. The conservative government has not been able to cut the total value of these welfare expenditures because such a policy would have faced stiffer opposition as compared with other social services. At the same time, the benefit per recipient family has declined as a result of more restrictive rules regarding the eligibility of those who applied for benefits. These social expenses are directed toward maintaining a minimum standard of living for the population. This is not indicative of the further upward development of the welfare state in the U.K. The recent years' developments provide more evidence of a gradual set-back for social policy and the welfare state. The focus of social policy has gradually shifted toward providing the minimum rather than expanding and upgrading social services.

In fact, the Thatcher government was committed to cut back social programs and to end what was referred to as a gradual drift to socialism. Certain programs were cutback for instance, spending on housing fell sharply during her administration. Nevertheless, certain income maintenance programs, including unemployment expenditures, continued to rise. Even the changes in the tax rates in the 1986 budget were beneficial to single parent families and, to some degree, to pensioners. But the high level income group also gained from the new tax policy due to the reduction in the highest rates of income tax. The losers, on the other hand, were the middle income groups, the majority of which were the working population (Dilnot and Stark, 1986). In contrast to the United States under the Reagan administration in which a number of welfare programs, particularly Aid to Families With Dependent Children, were cut back (Piven and Cloward, 1985), the parallel programs in the United Kingdom did not suffer from a drastic cut-back and total expenditures in these programs increased to a considerable degree. During the 1970's, the increasing costs of public assistance and welfare were entirely covered by the deficit spending of the government. However, the "fiscal responsibility" of the Thatcher administration meant that the rapid rise in the budget deficit had to be stopped and the burden of high costs of social welfare programs had to be shifted, in part, to the active members of the labor force (see Figures 5.5 and 5.6).

During the 1950's and 1960's the social benefits and public assistance allocated to the working population were more or less covered by their tax payments. The "overload" or "fiscal crisis" may have been a concern for the two recent decades of the 1970's and 1980's during which public assistance and welfare expenditures rose sharply. Due to the relative decline in the aggregate wage income, the government could not have forced the working population to cover this rising spending through additional tax payments. The Labor Government of 1974-1979 opted to cover this rising expenditure by accepting a higher (in nominal terms) budget deficit and an increasing borrowing requirement. But this increase was by no means out of proportion with respect to GNP growth.

Under the Thatcher Administration, the budget deficit remained stable (and even declined in real terms). The mounting unemployment rate, the increased number of low paying jobs, and the effort to force workers to accept low wages, made it impossible for the government to further intensify the pressure of taxation of the working population. It was therefore necessary for the government to impose a part of the burden of rising welfare expenses on the upper income families who were beneficiaries of the so-called economic prosperity achieved in this period (see Figure 5.5 and Table 5.3). But the increase in public assistance and welfare in this period has not been as substantial as to cause any problem for capital accumulation. Between 1980 and 1986, an additional value of 2.5 percent of GNP was absorbed by public assistance and welfare. Even if this whole value had been redistributed from capital to labor (or rather the poor), it would have caused no major problem given the gain business and upper income families made by government policies. In light of this analysis, we should suggest that the evidence for the United Kingdom supports neither the "overload" thesis nor the class struggle-induced crisis argument, such as the one suggested by Bowles and Gintis 1982.

So far we have particularly been concerned with theories of the welfare state. We have used the findings of our study to evaluate the implications of these theories for redistribution, accumulation, and the limits of the welfare state. In this section, we will compare the results of our study with the findings of the other major studies on the redistributive role of the welfare state. The major research projects in this area are conducted by Barna for 1937, Carter for 1948/49, Nicholson for various years during the 1950's and 1960's, and Stephenson for 1976. A more detailed evaluation of these studies was presented in Chapter three. The objective of this section is to compare our findings with the results of these studies.

In this research, I have been concerned with the impact of social policy on class inequality. These studies do not directly measure the redistribution of resources between major classes. Their findings are often summarized by income range. Their objective is to compare the distribution of initial and final incomes in order to find out how effective taxes and social welfare policies have been in redistributing incomes from families belonging to higher ranges of income to those with lower levels of income. They also pay attention to other family characteristics, such as the size of the family and its life cycle status.

The first step in redistribution studies is to calculate how incomes from wages, salaries, rent, interest, profit, and other sources are distributed between income receivers. The results are aggregated to produce data on the distribution of income between families and households. At this stage the effects of taxation (direct and indirect taxes and national insurance contributions) and social services (social security benefits, family allowances, education, health, etc.) on incomes are excluded. The resulting incomes are called "initial" or "pre-redistributional" incomes and are grouped in income ranges. In the second step the contribution of taxation and social services to initial incomes is taken into account. The post-welfare-state-activity incomes are refereed to as 'post-redistributional' incomes.

The third step involves the comparison of the distribution of initial and final income in order to measure the redistribution impact of the taxes and expenditures that have been included in the calculation.

These studies do not directly measure the outcome of the state tax and social policy for the working class which is the concern of our empirical project. There are also two other major methodological differences between our study and these studies. The redistributive studies assume that indirect taxes, or taxes on expenditure, are either paid by consumers (e.g., local rates and motor vehicle duties) or are fully reflected in the prices paid by consumers when buying commodities which are subject to sales taxes, customs, or excise taxes. In this research, taxes on expenditures such as sales taxes, excise taxes, and custom duties are assumed to have no direct effect on the net social wage received by the working population. To the extent that these taxes may have an influence on prices, they should be reflected in real wages of the workers which should be studied separately. Other forms of indirect taxes, such as rates and motor vehicle duties, are assigned to the working population in proportion to the share of labor income in total personal income.

In redistributive studies, the measurement of benefits from social expenditures such as education and public health is based on the assumption that all individuals of a particular category of given age and sex, or in a given type of school or college use the public services in equal proportions. In the previous Chapter, we challenged this assumption and explained in some detail why such an assumption would not be well-founded. The assumption that we have used is that benefits received by the working population from this type of public services are proportional to 'labor ratio' (i.e., the ratio of labor income over total personal income).

In spite of these major methodological differences, it is possible to compare our results with the findings of these redistributive studies. This is particularly the case because there is a major similarity between our methodology and the methodology adopted by these studies. Unlike the redistributive studies conducted in the United States, the British studies have made no attempt to estimate the benefits derived by households from expenditures on administration, defense, police, prisons, museums, libraries, parks, roads, and so on. In the case of administration, defense, police, and prison, the argument put forward is that these items do not bring any tangible benefits to households. Nicholson (1974) admits that other items, such as libraries, museums, parks, and roads, contribute to the enjoyment of families. But he disregards the benefits derived from these public goods due to the difficulty involved in their measurement.

We have not considered the first group as goods and services which can be consumed by the workers. Thus our methodology with regard to this group of expenditures is consistent with the method of measurement adopted in the redistributive studies. But we have tried to measure the benefits received by the working population for the second group of public expenditures.[1]

The conclusions derived from the redistributive studies are, in general, consistent with our findings. For families of the same type, the combination of direct and indirect taxes absorbs a stable proportion of income over a wide range of incomes. Taxation leads to some redistribution of income from families of small size to families of large size. But this redistributive result is not substantial. On the whole, the tax system is proportional (or even regressive) and not progressive. There are variations in tax payments by households within each income group, depending on the pattern of consumption and in particular how much they spend on drink and tobacco.

Social services, on the other hand, are progressive. However, social expenditures appear to have only a mildly progressive impact on "vertical inequality" but they have significant progressive effects on "horizontal inequality", mainly because they are more favorable to larger families. The study of Gini-Coefficient of inequality for initial and final incomes shows that a relatively significant degree of redistribution per annum was taking place during the fifties, sixties, and seventies.[2] But the contribution of taxation and social policy on income inequality has remained constant over time. It is interesting to note that Barna's estimate of 1937 showed a surprisingly similar degree of inequality of income before and after redistribution, and a similar reduction in inequality from benefits and taxes, to those documented by more recent studies by Nicholson. This means that post-redistribution incomes were as unequal in the post-war period as in the pre-war period (see Webb, 1971: 109).

In short, the findings of those studies do not support the view that the welfare state, so defined, is a significant factor in transforming the structure of inequality in British society (Wedderburn, 1965: 135). The expansion of welfare programs has not significantly modified the patterns of inequality created by the operation of the market economy. The growth of the benefits received by households from social expenditures has been accompanied by an increase in the proportion of incomes taken by taxation. At any one time welfare policies might have been effective in reducing inequality; but the major post-war changes in social policy, which have been so widely assumed to be egalitarian (and socialist in orientation), have made no significant contribution to the increased equality in incomes.

Our research is also concerned with the vertical redistribution of income. But it has focused more specifically on the redistributive contribution of state activities to class inequality. Our findings show a positive vertical redistribution of income for the post-war period. The working population has received more in benefits than they have paid in taxes. We have measured two versions of the net benefit (or net social wage). One includes Public Assistance and welfare and the second is net of this item. The latter has declined substantially over time but the former has remained relatively stable up to the mid-seventies and has increased in more recent years. This trend implies that for the majority of working class households, taxes have absorbed a larger proportion of their income than what they have received in benefits. Demographic changes and economic slow-down have resulted in a rise in unemployment and the number of households with very low incomes. This trend has led to the rising cost of welfare programs to provide a minimum subsistence for the poor. To finance these programs, the government has increased the tax burden of middle income working class households. This later conclusion is more or less in line with the findings of the redistributive studies. A careful review of the findings of these studies would lead to the conclusion that increased vertical redistribution was, in fact, concentrated on the lowest income households and the middle income families did not receive any significant net benefits, (see Chapter four and Web, 1971: 113).

Gough (1979) has put forward a thoughtful analysis of the social wage and its implications for accumulation.[3] His empirical analysis is comprised of two parts. In the first part, he gives an estimate of the flows between the personal and state sectors. His estimate is not based on a detailed measurement of the achievement of the various forms of taxes and expenditures. The other deficiency in his estimation is that as he himself admits, "it does not discriminate between households which receive their income from labor, from those whose income stems from property or from state benefits themselves" (p.108).

In the second part, he concentrates on the vertical redistribution of income between income groups. However, his entire analysis is based on the findings of the existing studies published by the CSO. He himself has not conducted any empirical research on the redistributive impact of social policy in Britain. His analysis in this section is more or less similar to what we discussed earlier in the context of the mainstream redistributive studies. The conclusion he arrives at is that "the return flow of welfare benefits to secure the reproduction of labor power falls far short of the taxes extracted from the working class"(p.160). This conclusion is mostly a guesswork because it is not based on any detailed measurement of the effects of social and tax policy. We have provided such a measurement and our results do not fully support his assertion with regard to the existence of a significantly negative net social wage. As we discussed earlier, the changes in the net social wage over time has been more complex than what he has suggested in his study.

So far our analysis has been based on the trend of the net social wage. It should be indicated that applying the second incidence assumption would substantially change the value of the net social wage, but not its pattern of change. With this assumption, the value of the net social wage will be negative for the entire period of our study (see Appendix IV). This result is in line with what Gough (1979) had suggested. What this shows is that taxes paid by workers exceed the benefits they have received from state activities.

In Appendix IV, we have presented three sets of Figures. The first set is similar to the Figures included in this Chapter. The only difference is the method we have used for the estimation of the indirect business taxes incidence. The second set is in line with the Figures in Appendix II in which the benefit/burden of the self-employed as partial workers is counted. The third set is similar to the Figures in Appendix III in which the share of the top managers in benefit and in taxes are deducted from the results. All these results in Appendix IV are based on the second incidence assumption for indirect business taxes.

What these results imply is that the taxes paid by the working population not only cover the benefits received by them, but also a part of the cost of general expenditures, such as military, policy, judiciary, infrastructure, and subsidies to the private sector. However, the trends of the net social wage using the alternative incidence assumptions are similar.

As Figures 1 and 2 in Appendix IV show, the net tax paid has increased over time. This is particularly true when we look at the trend of the net social wage during the 1970's and 1980's. The increase in the net tax paid by workers which had already started under the last Labor Government (1974-1979), continued to increase under Thatcher's government.

In this case, similar to the case with the first incidence assumption, the inclusion of public assistance and welfare in the benefits received by the working population changes the trend of the net social wage (or net tax) for the last two decades. As shown in Figures 2 and 3 in Appendix IV, the net tax (with public assistance included in benefits) has declined in this period. This is particularly true for the period after 1974, under the Conservative Government of Margaret Thatcher. As we explained before, this trend is the result of an increase in public assistance and welfare expenses at a much faster rate than before. This increase in public assistance is itself the result of an economic slow-down, high rate of unemployment, and poverty over this period. In other words, the decline in the net tax paid by working families is not indicative of any improvement in the quality and coverage of social programs. In fact, benefits per capita for the working population has declined due to more restrictive rules applied by the Thatcher Government.

To summarize, the expansion of the welfare state and social policy has faced strong barriers over the last decade in the U.K. The empirical evidence is not indicative of the expansion and increasing comprehensiveness of social services. It is rather indicative of a setback for the welfare state. But the setback, like the previous expansion, has been gradual and piecemeal. The working population has lost the rather substantial net benefits it used to receive during the post-war boom period. The growing rate of expansion of the public assistance and welfare expenses is, more than anything else, the cost of an economic slow-down and deterioration rather than the expansion of a social wage. The idea that the recent economic decline may have been caused by the growing welfare activities of the state is not supported by empirical evidence. It is rather the crisis of the welfare state which may have been resulted from the slow-down of the economy.

Notes

1. See chapter four for the method of measurement applied in this study.
2. For more detailed analysis of this issue, see chapter two.
3. For a more detailed analysis of Gough's study, see chapters two and three.

APPENDIX I

The estimation of the net social wage for the working population with and without adjustment for the self-employed and the top managers

Table 1.a
The measurement of the net social wage
(Adjusted for the top managers)

Social Expenditures				Including Self-Employment	
Group I	Total	Labor	Labor Adjusted	Labor	Labor Adjusted
Social Security Benefits	14689	14689	14689	14689	14689
Public Assistance and Welfare	10162		10162		10162
Group II					
Housing	6171	6171	6171	6171	6171
Education, Health	24382	16700	16700	18287	18287
Group III					
Public Utilities, Recreation	3687	2525	2525	2765	2765
Transport, Communication, Public Roads, and Lighting	3409	1704	1704	1866	1866
Total Social Benefits Received By Labor		41789	51951	43778	52074

Taxes	Total	Paid by Workers		Paid by Workers Adjusted for Self Employment	
Group I					
Taxes on Wages and Salaries	19866	19866		19866	
Tax Equivalent For Self-Employed				1903	
Social Security and Payroll Taxes	17086	17086		17086	
Group II					
Taxes on Property, Estate, Gift, Wealth, and Inheritance	9831				
- Taxes on Immovable Property Paid by Households	3641	2494		2730	
- Other Property Taxes, etc.	6190				
Other Taxes	254	173		190	
Total Taxes Paid by Labor		39619		41775	
Net Social Wage		2170	12332	2002	10299

*All values are in millions of pounds.

Notes

The Third Columns in the above table includes the workers benefits including Public Assistance and Welfare. This item is excluded from the second column. Categories of social expenditures are derived from various editions of The National Income and Expenditures of the U.K. To estimate the share of labor in Education, Health, Public Utilities, and Recreation, all of the categories in this group are multiplied by the "labor share" (0.68 for 1980). The share of households in the rest expenditures of group III is assumed to be proportional with the share of passenger cars gasoline consumption in the total gasoline consumption (0.73 for 1980). The result will be multiplied by the labor coefficient to obtain the labor share in the these expenditures. The data for taxes is obtained from several editions of OECD, Statistics of Revenue and Different editions of National Income and Expenditures of the U.K. To obtain the share of labor in group II taxes, the items of this group are multiplied by the "labor share". To measure the equivalents items for the self-employed, the "labor share" is adjusted to include the wage equivalent of the self-employed.

Table 1.b
The measurement of the net social wage
(Adjusted for the top managers)

Social Expenditures Group I	Total	Labor	Including Self-Employment		
			Labor Adjusted	Labor	Labor: Adjusted
Social Security Benefits	14689	14689	14689	14689	14689
Public Assistance and Welfare	10162		10162		10162
Group II					
Housing	6171	6171	6171	6171	6171
Education, Health	24382	14873	14873	16580	16580
Group III					
Public Utilities, Recreation	3687	2249	2249	2507	2507
Transport, Communication, Public Roads, and Lighting	3409	1518	1518	1692	1692
Total Social Benefits Received By Labor		39500	49662	41639	51801

Taxes Group I	Total	Paid by Workers	Paid by Workers Adjusted for Self-Employment	
Taxes on Wages and Salaries	19866	17795	17795	
Tax Equivalent For Self Employed			1903	
Social Security and Payroll Taxes	17086	17086	17086	
Group II				
Taxes on Property, Estate, Gift, Wealth, and Inheritance	9831			
Taxes on Immovable Property Paid by Households	3641	2221	2476	
Other Property Taxes, etc.	6190			
Other Taxes	254	155	173	
Total Taxes Paid by Labor		37257	39433	
Net Social Wage		2243	12332	2207	10321

Notes

By excluding the product of the number of administrative and managerial personnel by the average earnings of the highest decile, the labor ratio is adjusted to exclude the share of top managers from labor benefits and taxes.

Table 2.a
Benefits and taxes paid by labor
(Adjusted for the self employed)

Year	Taxes Paid By Labor	Social Benefits Received By Labor	Net Social Wage	Net Social Wage without Public Assistance
1953	1277	2572	1295	817
1954	1353	2626	1272	788
1955	1520	2825	1305	805
1956	1711	3091	1380	858
1957	1873	3216	1343	798
1958	2152	3452	1300	741
1959	2240	3689	1449	854
1960	2434	3987	1554	919
1961	2779	4390	1611	954
1962	3095	4670	1575	876
1963	3235	5147	1912	1156
1964	3601	5765	2164	1362
1965	3779	6524	2745	1888
1966	5092	6726	1634	709
1967	5680	7603	1924	830
1968	7043	8370	1327	65
1969	7354	8133	779	-712
1970	8377	10069	1693	75
1971	8806	11044	2237	408
1972	9445	12897	3451	1304
1973	10615	15307	4691	2407
1974	13733	20146	6413	3576
1975	19876	26031	6154	2299
1976	23966	30547	6580	1702
1977	26841	33589	6748	1158
1978	29123	38303	9180	2066
1979	33806	44430	10624	1944
1980	41594	53933	12338	2154
1981	46273	61371	15097	1326
1982	52805	67191	14386	-3060
1983	52849	73014	20165	1056
1984	55432	77101	21669	448
1985	58209	81769	23560	-327
1986	64630	88835	24204	-1423

Table 2.b
Benefits and taxes paid by labor
(Adjusted for the self employed)

Year	Taxes Paid By Labor	Social Benefits Received By Labor	Net Social Wage	Net Social Wage without Public Assistance
1953	1277	2572	1295	817
1954	1353	2626	1272	788
1955	1520	2825	1305	805
1956	1711	3091	1380	858
1957	1873	3216	1343	798
1958	2152	3452	1300	741
1959	2240	3689	1449	854
1960	2434	3987	1554	919
1961	2779	4390	1611	954
1962	3095	4670	1575	876
1963	3235	5147	1912	1156
1964	3601	5765	2164	1362
1965	3779	6524	2745	1888
1966	5092	6726	1634	709
1967	5680	7603	1924	830
1968	7043	8370	1327	65
1969	7354	8133	779	-712
1970	8377	10069	1693	75
1971	8806	11044	2237	408
1972	9445	12897	3451	1304
1973	10615	15307	4691	2407
1974	13733	20146	6413	3576
1975	19876	26031	6154	2299
1976	23966	30547	6580	1702
1977	26841	33589	6748	1158
1978	29123	38303	9180	2066
1979	33806	44430	10624	1944
1980	41594	53933	12338	2154
1981	46273	61371	15097	1326
1982	52805	67191	14386	-3060
1983	52849	73014	20165	1056
1984	55432	77101	21669	448
1985	58209	81769	23560	-327
1986	64630	88835	24204	-1423

Table 2.c
Benefits and taxes paid by labor
(Adjusted for the self employed and top managers)

Year	Taxes Paid By Labor	Social Benefits Received By Labor	Social Benefits Received By Labor	Net Social Wage	Net Social Benefit without Public Assistance
1953	1244	2011.91	2523	1279	801
1954	1317	2054.06	2574	1256	772
1955	1480	2227.23	2773	1293	793
1956	1667	2455.91	3031	1365	843
1957	1821	2549.94	3149	1327	782
1958	2096	2768.00	3387	1291	732
1959	2181	2959.78	3616	1435	840
1960	2365	3203.01	3911	1546	911
1961	2699	3572.46	4283	1584	927
1962	3005	3799.91	4558	1553	854
1963	3139	4208.22	5019	1880	1124
1964	3490	4761.85	5615	2124	1322
1965	4095	5445.91	6353	2258	1401
1966	4929	5588.84	6560	1631	706
1967	5501	6259.84	7432	1931	837
1968	6799	6832.04	8159	1361	99
1969	7106	6335.77	7909	804	-687
1970	8083	8092.83	9807	1725	107
1971	8465	8806.26	10704	2239	410
1972	9082	10749.45	12533	3451	1304
1973	10180	12979.72	14886	4706	2422
1974	13163	17309.24	19640	6477	3640
1975	18964	22024.74	25204	6239	2384
1976	22802	25605.88	29554	6753	1882
1977	25574	27892.84	32439	6866	1287
1978	27765	31103.59	37223	9458	2352
1979	32204	35655.09	42957	10753	2082
1980	39433	43526.38	51801	12369	2207
1981	43791	44600.89	58524	14733	1351
1982	49849	46740.29	64305	14456	-2553
1983	49637	50599.90	69558	19921	1274
1984	48332	52682.53	73346	25014	4279
1985	54216	54657.59	77678	23462	90
1986	59826	59845.15	83988	24162	-902

APPENDIX II

The estimation of the net social wage for the working population and the self-employed

The Figures in this appendix are similar to the ones presented in Chapter five. The only difference is that the results in this section are adjusted to include both benefits received and taxes paid by the self-employed. The self-employed include proprietors and partners in non-corporate business and they are treated partly as workers and partly as owners of capital. In the estimation of the benefit/burden of the working population the wage equivalent of the self-employed is also taken into account. The more detailed methodology is explained in Chapter four.

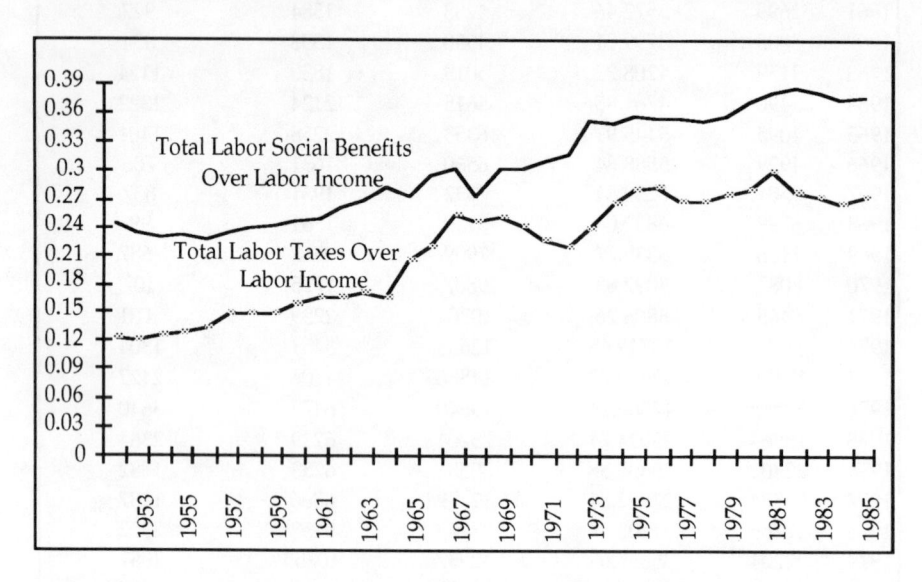

Figure II.1　Total labor taxes over labor income and total social benefits over labor income (self employed and public assistance included)

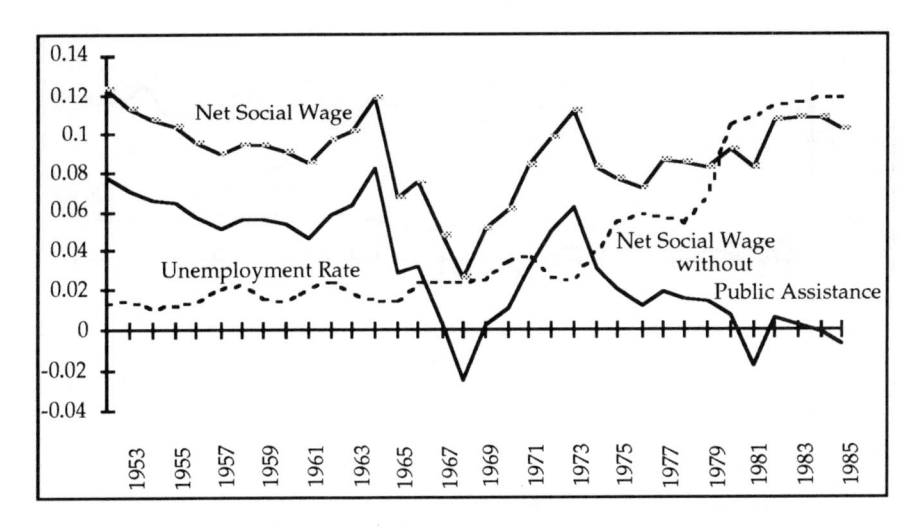

Figure II.2 Net social wage ratio adjusted for self employed and unemployment rate

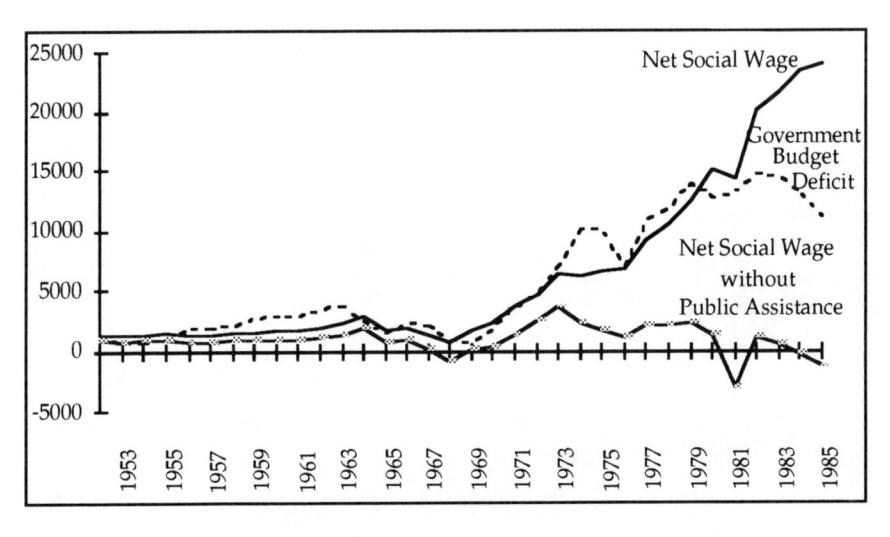

Figure II.3 Government budget deficit and net social wage (with and without public assistance)

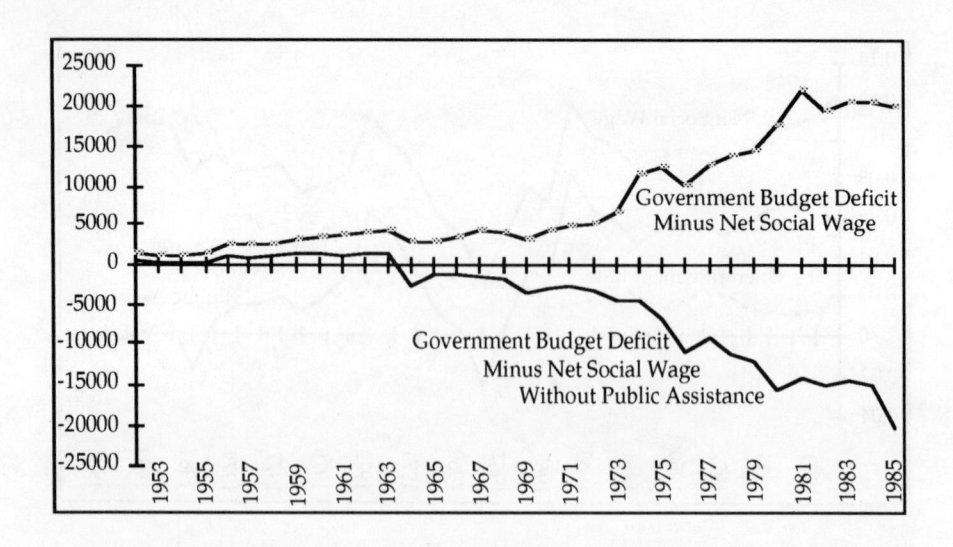

Figure II.4 Government budget deficit minus net social wage (with and without public assistance)

Appendix III

The trend of the net social wage for the working population and the self-employed: Excluding the share of the top managers

The results in this appendix are adjusted to exclude the benefits received and taxes paid by top managers. In the measurement of the "labor share" the attempt is made to exclude the salaries of top managers and executives. This new value of the labor share is used to estimate the benefit/burden of the working population and the net social wage. The concept of the working population in this section includes the self-employed to the extent that they can be treated as workers. The more detailed methodology is discussed in Chapter three.

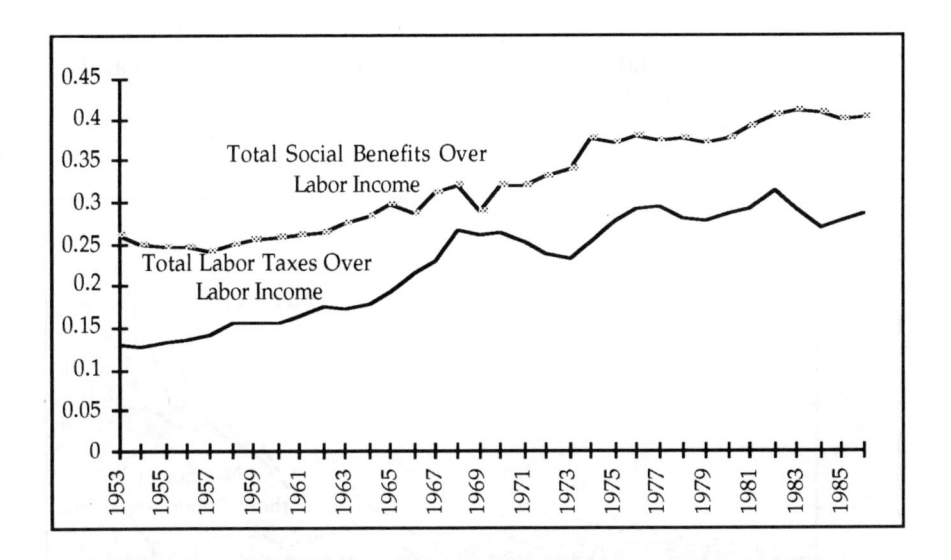

Figure III.1 Total labor taxes over labor income and total labor social benefits over labor income

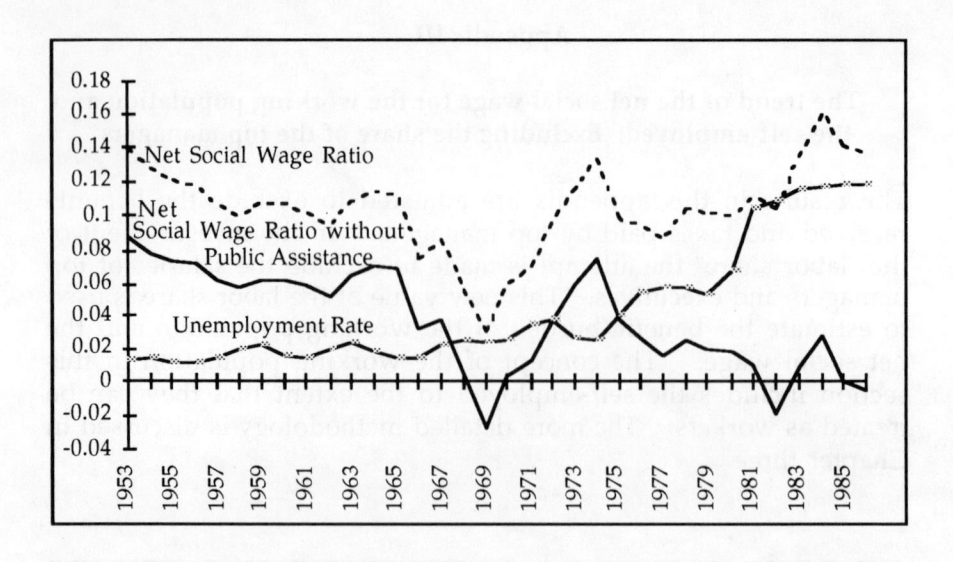

Figure III.2 Net social wage ratio (adjusted for top managers and self employed and unemployment rate)

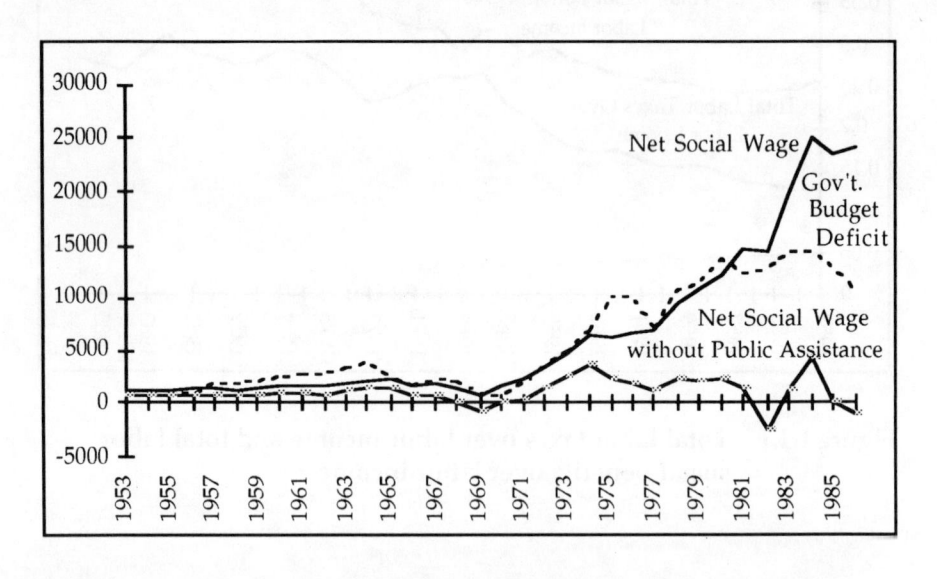

Figure III.3 Government Budget deficit and net social wage (with and without public assistance)

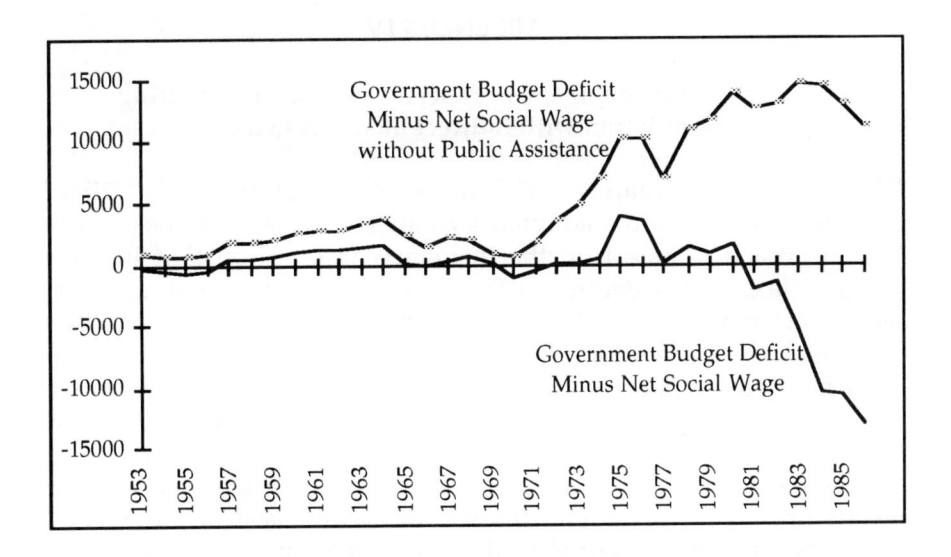

Figure III.4 Government budget deficit minus net social wage (with and without public assistance)

APPENDIX IV

The estimation of the net social wage for the working population with indirect business taxes

To estimate the share of the working population in indirect business taxes we have adopted two alternative approaches. The first approach is based on the incidence assumption that indirect business taxes are a deduction from profit (or surplus value). The second approach is based on the assumption that indirect business taxes are fully reflected in final prices and their burden is shifted to households as consumers of the final products. (See Chapter three for further explanation). In this appendix all the results presented in Chapter four, Appendix II, and Appendix III are reproduced using the second incidence assumption for indirect business taxes. The results presented in Appendixes V and VI are based on the second incidence assumption but with the adjustments for the share of the self-employed and the top managers.

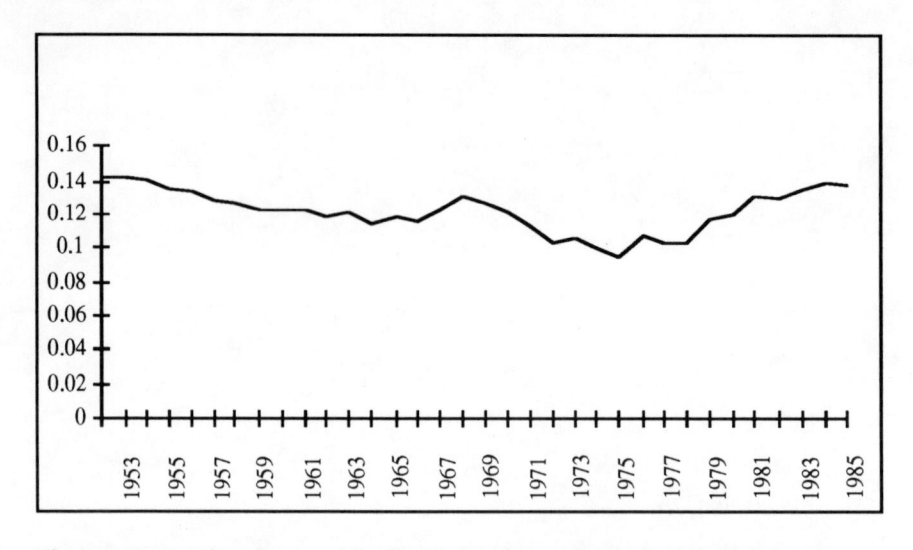

Figure IV.1 The share of indirect business taxes in labor income

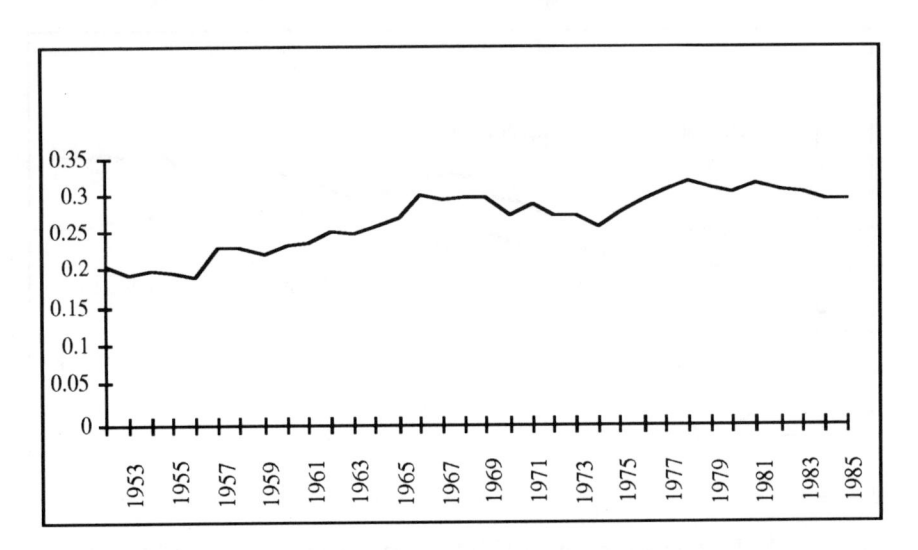

Figure IV.2 The share of social security and payroll taxes in total labor taxes (indirect business taxes included)

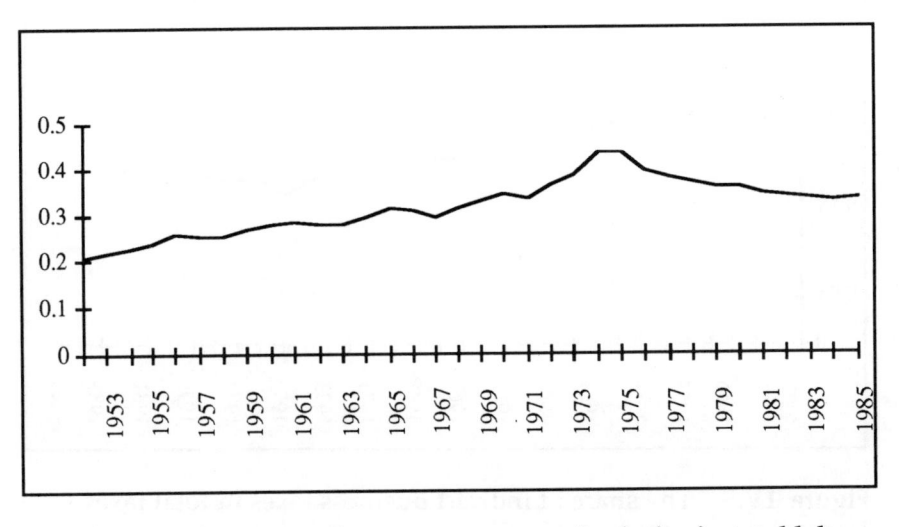

Figure IV.3 The share of taxes on wages and salaries in total labor taxes (Indirect business taxes included)

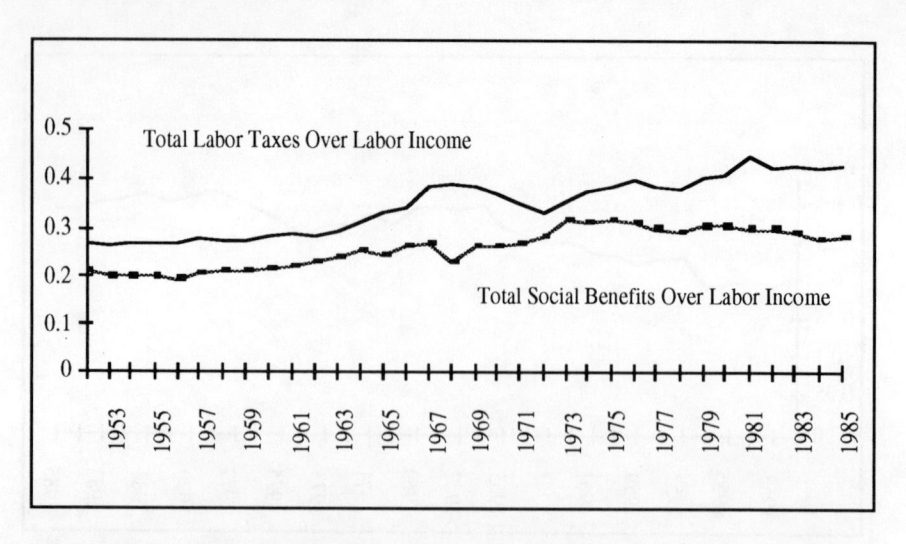

Figure IV.4 The share of total labor taxes (with indirect business taxes) in labor income and total labor social benefits in labor income

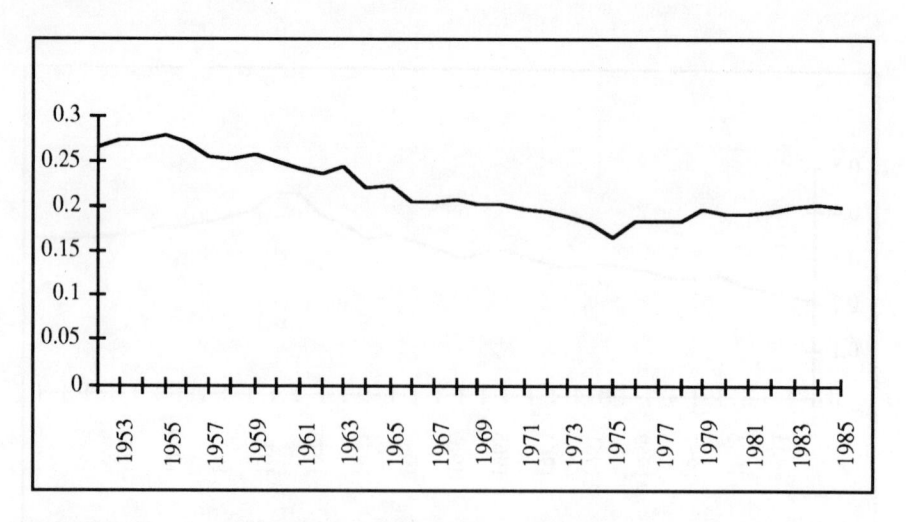

Figure IV.5 The share of indirect business taxes in total taxes

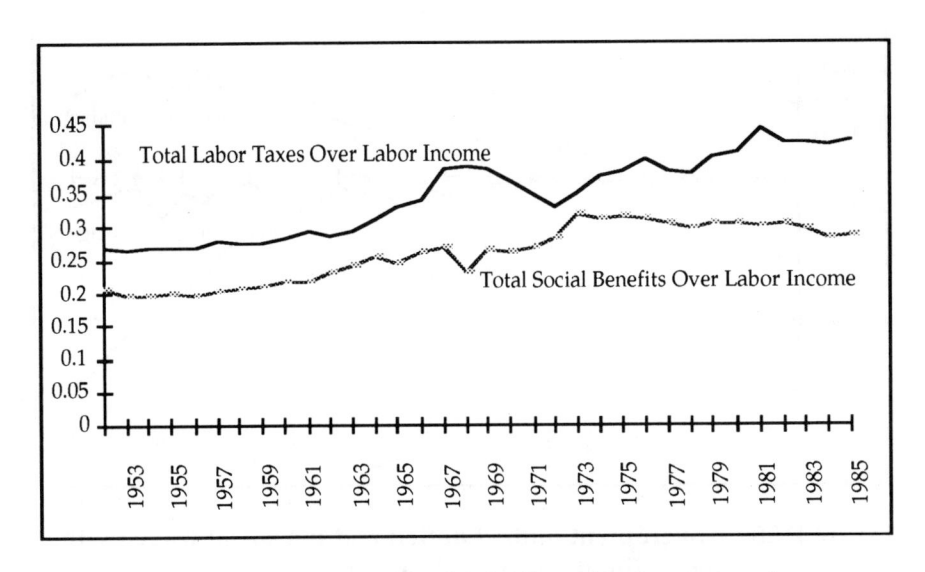

Figure IV.6 Total labor taxes (with indirect business taxes) over labor income and total labor social benefits over labor income

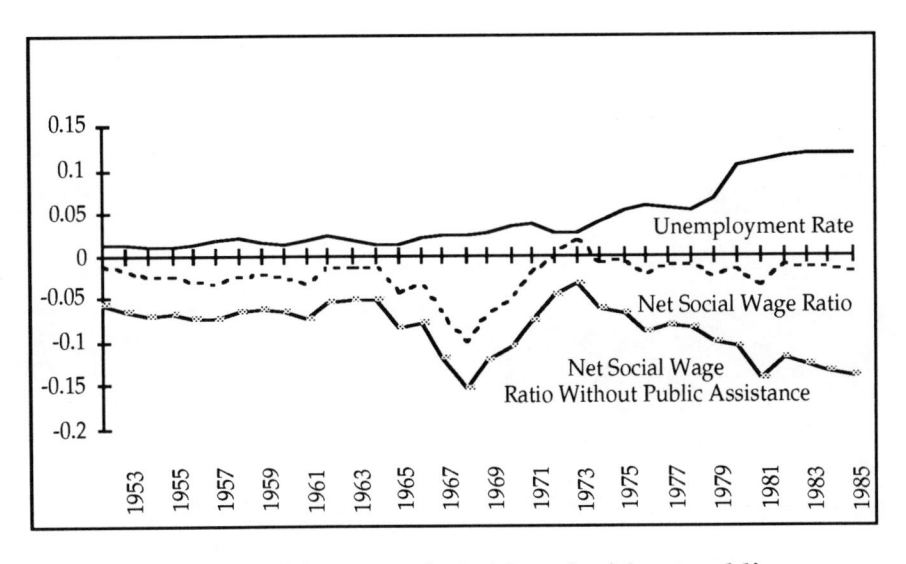

Figure IV.7 Net social wage ratio (with and without public assistance and unemployment rate)

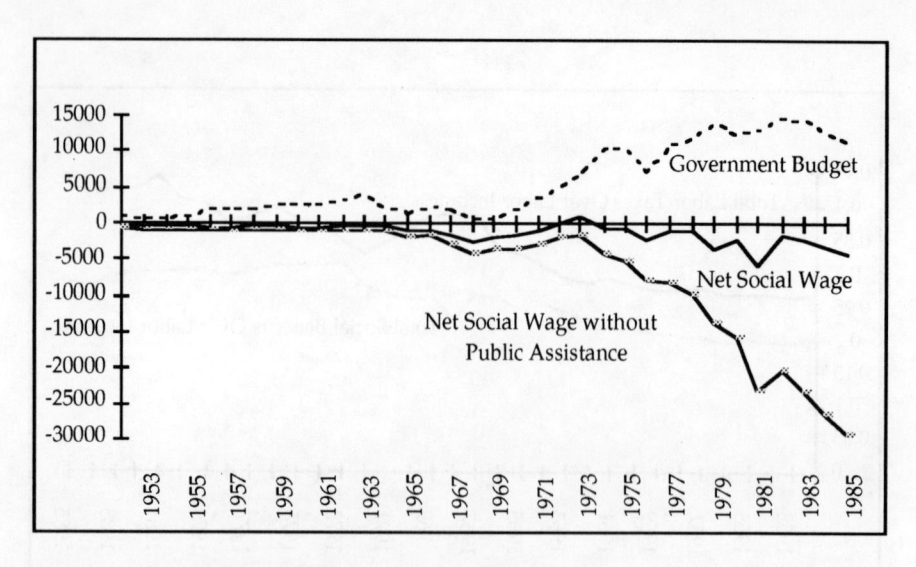

Figure IV.8 Government budget deficit and net social wage (with and without public assistance)

APPENDIX V

The estimation of the net social wage for the working population and the self-employed
(Indirect business taxes included)

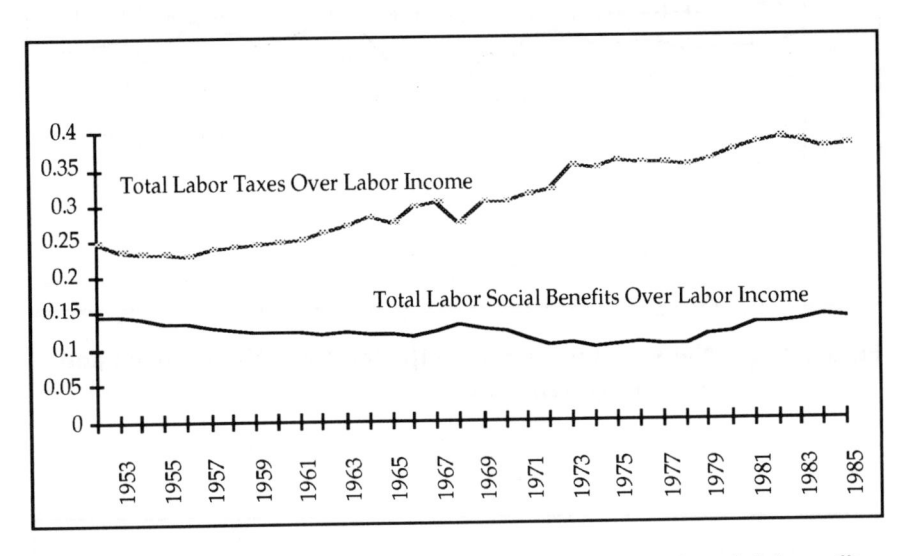

Figure V.1 Total labor taxes over labor income and social benefits over labor income (self employed and public assistance included)

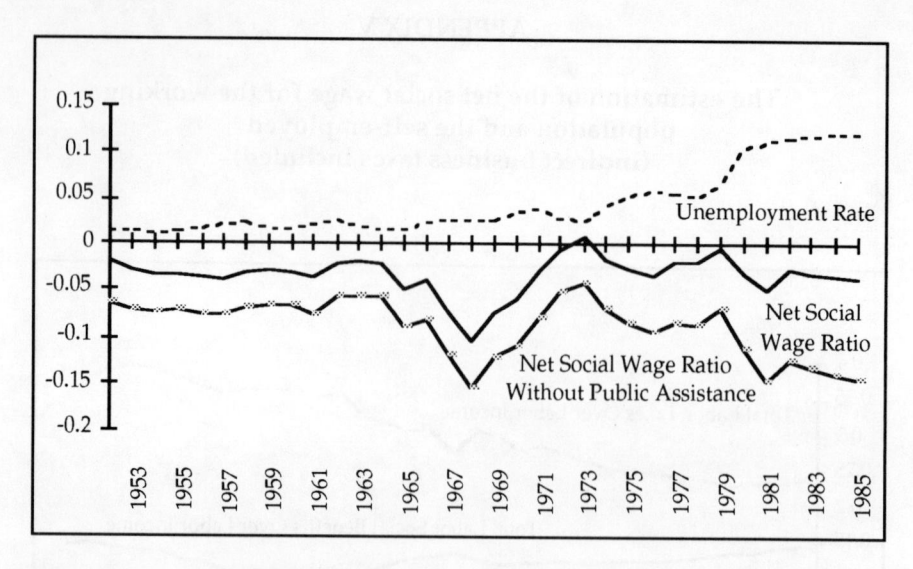

Figure V.2 Net social wage ratio adjusted for self-employed and unemployment rate

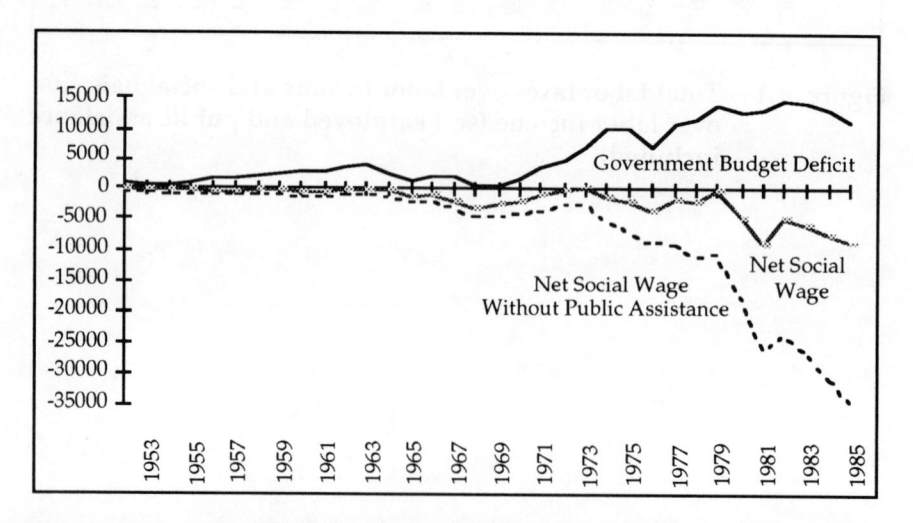

Figure V.3 Government budget deficit and net social wage (with and without public assistance)

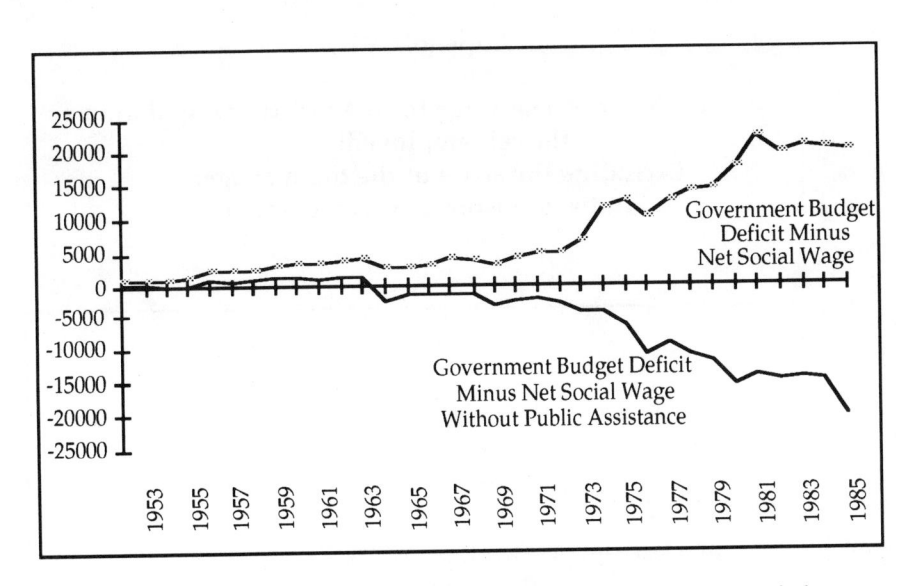

Figure V.4 Government budget deficit minus net social wage (with and without public assistance)

Appendix VI

The trend of the net social wage for the working population and the self employed:
Excluding the share of the top managers
(Indirect business taxes included)

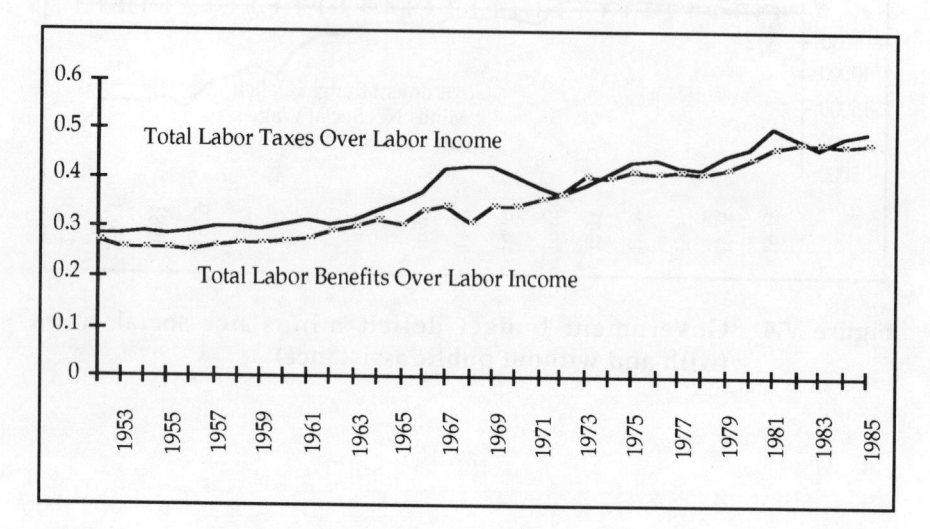

Figure VI.1 Total labor taxes over labor income and total labor social benefits over labor income

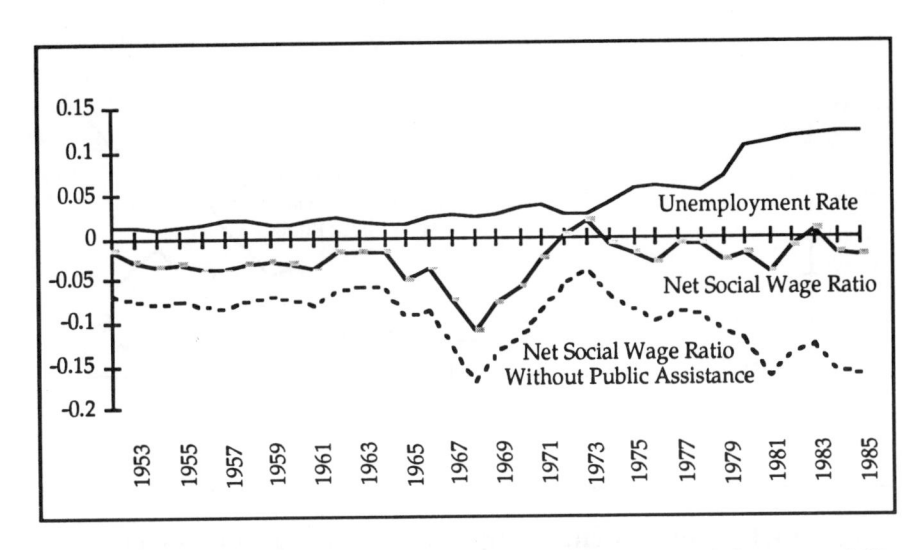

Figure VI.2 Net social wage ratio (with and without public assistance and self-employed) and unemployment rate (adjusted for top managers)

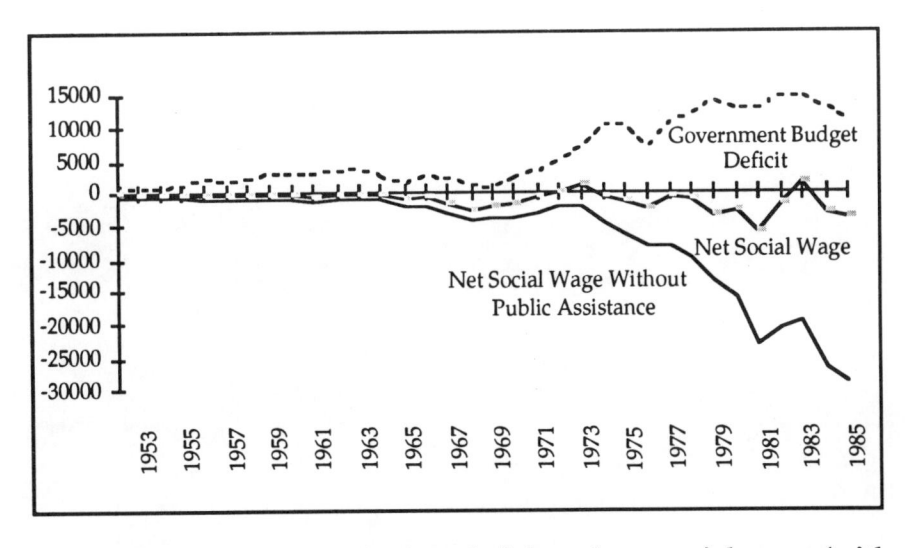

Figure VI.3 Government budget deficit and net social wage (with and without public assistance)

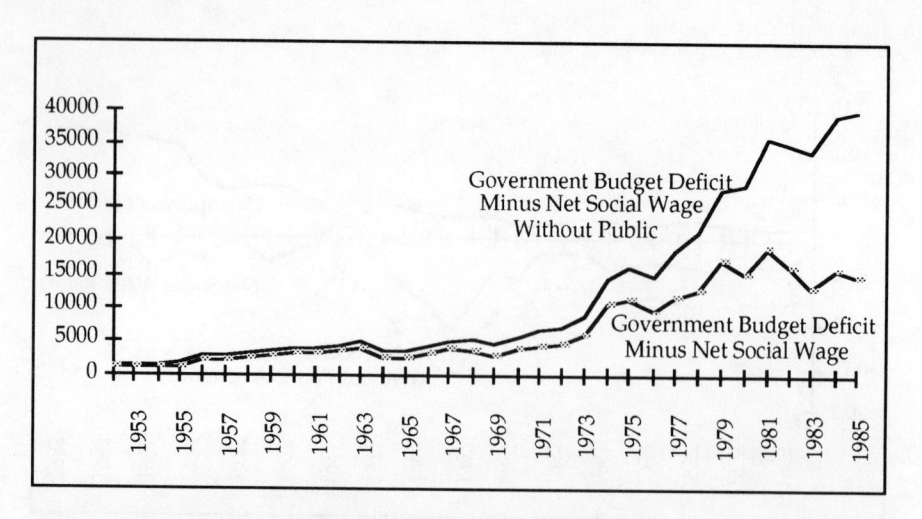

Figure VI.4 Government budget deficit minus net social wage (with and without public assistance and self employed) adjusted for top managers

Bibliography

Alber, Jens. (1982) Government Responses to the Challenge of Unemployment: The Development of Unemployment Insurance in Western Europe, in Peter Flora and Arnold Heidenheimer (ed.), *The Development of Welfare State in Europe and America*. New Brunswick. Transaction Books.

Anderson, Perry. (1980) *Lineages of the Absolutist State*, London: Verso.

Atkinson, Anthony and Joseph Stiglitz. (1980) *Lectures On Public Finance*, New York: McGraw-Hill.

Bacon, Robert and Walter Eltis. (1976) *Britain's Economics Problems: Too Few Producers*, London.

Bakker, Isabella. (1986) *The Reproduction of the Working Population in Canada*. Ph.D Dissertation. Department of Economics, New School for Social Research.

Bendis, Reinhard. (1967) Tradition and Modernity Reconsidered, Comparative Studies in *Society and History*, 9: 292-346.

Bottomore, Tom. (1983) *A Dictionary of Marxist Thought*, London: Basil Blackwell.

Bowles. S and H. Gintis. (1982) The Crisis of Liberal Democratic Capitalism, in *Politics and Society*, vol. II, no.1.

Briggs, Asa. (1961) The Welfare State in Historical Perspective, in *European Journal of Sociology*, 2, pp. 221-258.

Briggs, Asa. (1960) The Welfare State in Historical Perspective, *European Journal of Sociology*, Vol.II.

Brittan, S. (1971) *Steering the Economy*, Harmondsworth: Penguin.

Buchanon, James and Marilyn Flowers. (1980) *The Public Finance*, New York: Irwin.

Carter, A. M. (1955) The *Redistribution of Income in Post-War Britain*, New Haven: Yale University Press.

Cartwright, A. (1964) *Human Relations and Hospital Care*, Routledge & Kegan Paul.
Cashmore, E. Ellis. (1989) United Kingdom? Class, Race and Gender Since the War, London: Unwin Hyman.
Caves, R.E. et al. (1968) *Britain's Economic Prospects*, Washington, D.C: Brookings Institution.
Chambliss, William. (1964) A Sociological Analysis of the Law of Vagrany, *Social Problems* 12, No.1, Summer.
Collier, David and Richard Messick. (1975) Prerequisites Versus Diffusion: Testing Alternative Explanations of Social Security Adoption, *American Political Science Review*, 69: 1299-1315.
Chrystal, K.A. (1979) *Controversies in British Macroeconomics*. Oxford: Philip Allan.
Crouch, Colin (edit.). (1979) *State and Economy in Contemporary Capitalism*. London: Croom Helm Pp.13-53.
C.S.O; Abstract of Statistics of Great Britain, several editions.
C.S.O; The Transportation Abstract of the U.K, several editions.
DeBrunhoff, Suzanne. (1978) *The State, Capital and Economic Policy*, London: Pluto Press.
Dilnot, A.W. and G.K.Stark. (1986) The Distributional Consequences of Mrs. Thatcher, in *Fiscal Studies*, Vol.7, no.2, May (1986)
Disney, R. (1982) "Theorising the Welfare State: the Case of Unemployment Insurance in Britain," *Journal of Social Policy*, Vol. 11, No.1.
Dobb, Maurice. (1976) *Studies in the Development of Capitalism*, New York: International Publishers.
Doyal, L. (1979) *The Political Economy of Health*, Plato.
Fazeli, Rafat and Reza Fazeli. (1984) *The Distributive Effects of the State Activities on the Working Class: A Comparative Study of the U.S. and the U.K.*, Unpublished Research Paper. Department of Economics, New School for Social Research.
Fine, B., and Harris, L., (1976a) State Expenditures in Advance Capitalism: A Critique, *New Left Review*, No. 98, July/August.
Fine, B., and Harris, L., (1976b) "The British Economy since March (1975)", *CSEB* IV.12 (October).
Fine, B., and Harris, L., (1976c) Controversial Issues in Marxist Economic Theory, in Ralph Milliband and John Saville (eds.) *The Socialist Register*.
Flora, Peter and Arnold Heidenheimer. (1982) The Historical Care and Changing Boundries of th Welfare State in Flora, Peter and Arnold Heidenheimer (eds.), *The Development of Welfare State in Europe and America*. New Brunswick. Transaction Books.

Flora, Peter and Arnold Heidenheimer. (1982) Introduction in Peter Flora and Arnold Heidenheimer edit. *The Development of Welfare States in Europe and America*, New Brunswick: Transaction Books.

Flora, Peter and Jens Alber. (1982) Modernization, and the Development of Welfare States in Western Europe, in Peter Flora and Arnold Heidenheimer (edit.), *The Development of Welfare State in Europe and America.* New Brunswick. Transaction Books.

Friedman, Kathi. (1981) *Legitimation of Social Rights and the Western Welfare State*, Chapel Hill: University of North Carolina Press.

Friedman, Milton and Rose Friedman. (1980) *Free to Choose*, Harmondsworth: Penguin.

Friedman, Milton. (1977) From Galbraith to Economic Freedom. London: Institute of Economic Affairs.

Galbraith, J. K. (1967) *The New Industrial State*, London: Hamish Hamilton.

Gamble, Andrew. (1981) *Britain in Decline*, Boston: Beacon Press.

George, Victor and Paul Wilding. (1984) *The Impact of Social Policy*, London: Routledge & Kegan Paul.

George, Victor. (1973) *Social Security and Society*, London: Routledge & Kegan Paul.

Gilbert, Geoffrey. (1988) Toward the Welfare State: Some British Views on the Right to Subsistence, 1768-1834, *Review of Social Economy*, No.2, October.

Glyn and Sutcliff. (1971) *British Capitalism, Workers and the Profit Squeeze*, London.

Gough, Ian. (1979) *The Political Economy of the Welfare State*, London: MacMillan.

Hall, A. Peter. (1986) The State and Economic Decline in Bernard Elbaum and William Lazonick (eds.), *The Decline of the British Economy*, Oxford: Clarendon Press.

----------.(1983) Patterns of Economic Policy: *An Oranizational Approach*, in David Held (ed.) States and Societies, New York: New York University Press.

Halsey, A., A.Health, and J. Judge. (1980) *Origins and Destinations*, Clarendon Press.

Hart, J.T. (1975) The Inverse Case Law, in C. Cox and A.Mead (eds), *A Sociology of Medical Practice*, Collier-Macmillan.

Heclo, Hugh. (1974) *Modern Social Politics in Britain and Sweden: From Relief to Income Maintenance*, New Haven and London: Yale University Press.

Heilbroner, Robert. L and James K. Galbraith. (1990) *Understanding Macroeconomics*, Englewood Cliffs, N.J.: Prentice Hall.

H.M Treasury, *National Income and Expenditures of the United Kingdom*, various editions.

Heidenheimer, Arnold J. (1982) Education and Social Security Entitlements in Europe and America, in Peter Flora and Arnold Heidenheimer (eds.), *The Development of Welfare State in Europe and America*. New Brunsweek. Transaction Books.

Hicks, Ursula K. (1956) "The Terminology of Tax Analysis", *Economic Journal*, March.

Holloway, John and Sol Piciotto. (1978) *State and Capital*, London: Arnold.

Hayek, F. A. (1978) *New Studies in Philosophy, Politics, Economics and History of Ideas*, Chicago: University of Chicago Press.

ILO. Yearbook of Statistics, Various Editions.

Jessop, Bob. (1980) The Transformation of the State in Post-War Britain. in Richard Scase (ed.) (1980) The State in Western Europe. New York: St. Martin's.

----------. (1977) Recent Theories of the Capitalist State, *Cambridge Journal of Economics* 1(14).

Janowitx, Morris. (1976) Social Control of the Welfare State, New York: Elsevier.

Jones, F.E. (1978) Our Manufacturing Industry-the Missing 100,000 Pounds Million, *National Westminster Bank Quarterly Review*, May 8-17.

Jordon, W. K. (1959) *Philanthropy in England, 1480-1660*, London: Allen and Unwin.

Joseph, Sirkeith. (1976) *Monetarism Is Not Enough*, London: Centre for Policy Studies.

Kerr, Clark et al., (1973) *Industrialization and Industrial Man*, Harmondsworth: Penguin.

King, Anthony. (1975) *Overload: Problems of Governing in the 1970's*, Political Studies, 23: 283-96

Klein, Rudolf. (1976) The Politics of Public Expenditures: American Theory and British Practice, *British Journal of Political Science*. 6, pp. 401-432.

Kotz, David M. (1990) A Comparative Analysis of the Theory of Regulation and the Social Structure of Accumulation Theory, *Science and Society*, Vol.54, No.1, Spring.

Krieger, Joel. (1986) *Reagan, Thatcher, and the Politics of Decline*, Oxford: Oxford University Press.

Kudrle, Robert T. and Theodora R. Marmor. (1982) The Development of Welfare States in North America, in Peter Flora and Arnold Heidenheimer (eds.), *The Development of Welfare State in Europe and America.* New Brunsweek. Transaction Books.
Kuhnle, Stein. (1982) The Growth of Social Insurance Programs in Scandinavia: Outside Influences and Internal Factors, in Peter Flora and Arnold Heidenheimer (eds.), *The Development of Welfare State in Europe and America.* New Brunswick. Transaction Books.
Lockwood, David. (1964) Social Integration and System Integration, in George K. Zollschan and Walter Hirsch, *Exploitations in Social Change*, London: Routledge and Kegan Paul.
Los Angles Times. (1990, July, 17)
Lowe, Rodney. (1993) *The Welfare State in Britain Since 1945*, New York: St. Martin's Press.
Mandel, Ernest. (1978) *The Second Slump*, London: NLR.
Marshall, Dorothy. (1926) *The English Poor in the Eighteenth Century*, London: George Routledge and Sons.
Marshall, T. H. (1981) The Right to Welfare and Other Essays, New York: The Free Press.
Marshall, T. H. (1965) *Class, Citizenship, and Social Devlopment.* Garden City, N.Y.: Anchor Books.
Marshall, T. H. (1964) Class Citizenship and Social Development, New York: Doubleday & Company, Inc.
Marx, Karl. (1977) *Capital*, vols. I-III, Moscow: International Publishers.
McCrone, David, Brian Elliott and Frank Bechehoffer. (1989) Corportaism and the New Right, in Richard Scase ed. *Industrial Societies*, London: Unwin Hyman.
Middlemas, Keith. (1979) *Politics in Industrial Society*, London: Deutsch.
Mishra, Ramish. (1981) *Society and Social Policy*, London: MacMillan.
----------. (1984) *The Welfare State in Crisis*, New York: St Martin's.
Musgrave, Richard and Peggy Musgrave. (1984) *Public Finance in Theory and Practice*, New York: McGraw-Hill.
Musgrave, Richard et al. (1974) 'The Distribution of Fiscal Budens and Benefits', *Public Finance Quarterly*, July.
Navarro, V. (1976) *Medicine Under Capitalism*, Prodist/Croom Helm.
----------. (1979) *Class Stuggle, The State and Medicine*, Martin Robertson.

Nicholson, J.L. (1974) The Distribution and Redistribution of Income in the United Kingdom, in Dorothy Wedderburn, ed. *Poverty, Inequality and Class Structure*, Cambridge: Cambridge University Press.

OECD. (1985) 'The Role of the Public Sector', OECD. *Economic Studies*, No. 4, Spring.

OECD. (1981) *The Welfare State in Crisis*.

OECD. (1976) Public Expenditure On Income Maintenance Programmes. Paris: OECD.

O'Connor, James. (1973) *The Fiscal Crisis of the State*, New York: St.Martin's.

Offe, Clause. (1982) Contradictions of the Welfare State. Cambridge, MA: The MIT Press.

Pechman, Joseph A. and Benjamin A. Okner. (1974) *Who Bears the Tax Burden?* Washington, D. C.: Brookings Institution.

Pinker, Robert. (1981) Introduction, in T.H. Marshall. *The Right to Welfare and Other Essays*, New York: The Free Press.

Pinker, Robert. (1979) The Idea of Welfare. London: Heinemann.

Piven, Frances Fox and Richard Cloward (1985) *The New Class War*, New York: Pantheon Books.

Quadagno, Jill. (1984) Welfare Capitalism and the Social Security Act of 1935, *American Sociological Review*, 49: 632-47.

Ricardo, David. (1981) *On the Principles of Political Economy and Taxation, Piero Sraffa ed., Vol.I,* Cambridge: Cambridge University Press.

Rimlinger, G.V. (1971) *Welfare Policy and Industrilization in Europe, America and Russia*, New York: Wiley.

Saville, John. (1965) Labour and Income Redistribution, in Ralph Miliband and John Saville eds. *The Socialist Register*, New York: Monthly Review Press.

Saville, John. (1957-58) The Welfare State: A Historical Approach, *The New Reasoner*, No.3, Winter.

Schweinitz, K. de. (1961) *England's Road to Social Security*, Pennsylvania: University of Pennsylvania Press.

Scott, Kerry. (1982) The Rise of Keynesian Economics: Britain (1940-64) in David Held(ed.) (1983) *States and Societies*. New York: N.Y.U.Press.

Semmler, Willi. (1982) *Private Production and the Public Sector*, Paper for the 95th Annual Meeting of the American Economic Association, New York: December 30, 1982.

----------.(1983) On the Classical Theory of Taxation, an Analysis of Tax Incidence in a Linear Production Model, *Metroeconomica*, 25, Feb.

Shaikh, Anwar.(1983) *The Current Economic Crisis: Causes and Implications*, New School for Social Research.

---------. (1980) *National Income Accounts and Marxian Categories*, Unpublished Paper, New School for Social Research.

---------. (1978a) An Introduction to the History of Crisis Theories, in U.S. Capitalism in Crisis, New York: URPE.

---------. (1978b) Political Economy and Capitalism: Notes on Dobbs Theory of Crisis, *Cambridge Journal of Economics*, no. 2.

--------- and E. Ahmet Tonak. (1987) The Welfare State and the Myth of Social Wage in *Imperiled Economy*, Book I, Salt Lake City: URPE.

Skocpol, Theda and John Ikenberry. (1983) The Political Formation of American Welfare State, in Historical and Comparative Perspective, *Comparative Social Register*, Vol.6.

Skocpol, Theda. (1980) *States and Social Revolutions*, Cambridge: Cambridge University Press.

Smelser, Neil. (1964) Toward a Theory of Modernization in Etzioni and Etzioni, eds. *Social Change*, New York: Basic Books.

Stephenson. G. A. (1978) The Effects of Taxes and Benefits on Household Income, (1976, Economic Trends.

Stiglitz, Joseph. (1986) *Economics of the Public Sector*, New York: W.W.Norton.

Sweezy, Paul et al. (1976) The Transition from Feudalism to Capitalism, London: *NLR*.

Tawney, R. H. (1964) *Equality*, London: Allen and Unwin.

Tawney, R. H. (1913) *Poverty as an Industrial Problem*, London: The Ratan Tata Foundation Memoranda On Problems of Poverty, II.

Thompson, E. P. (1971) The Moral Economy of the English Crowd in the Eighteenth Century, *Past and Present*, No. 50, February.

Thompson, E. P. (1963) *The Making of the English Working Class*, New York: Vintage Books.

Tilly, Charles. (1978) *From Mobilization to Revolution*, Mass: Addison-Wesley Publishing Co.

Tomlinson, Jim. (1981) Was Economic Policy Ever Keynesian?, *Economy and Society*, vol.10, no.1.

Tonak, E. Ahmet. (1987) The U.S. Welfare State and the Working Class, (1952-1980) *Review of Radical Political Economy* 191: 47-72.

Tonak, E. Ahmet. (1984) *A Conceptualization of State Revenues and Expenditures: U.S., (1952-1980)* Ph.D. Dissertation. Department of Economics, New School for Social Research.

U.S. Department of Commerce. (1981) Statistical Abstract of the United States, Bureau of Census.

Walley, Sir John. (1972) *Social Security*, London: C. Knight.

Webb, Adrian L. (1971) *Income Redistribution and the Welfare State*, London: Bell & Sons.

Wedderburn, Dorothy. (1974) Poverty, Inequality and Class Structure, Cambridge: Cambridge University Press.

Wedderburn, Dorothy. (1965) Facts and Theories of the Welfare State, in Ralph Milliband and John Saville eds. *The Socialist Register*: Monthly Review press.

Weed, Frank J. (1979) Industrialization and Welfare System, *International Journal of Comparative Sociology*, 20, 3-4.

West, R. and C. Lowe. (1976) Reginal Variations in Need for and Provision and Use of Child Health Services in England and Wales, *British Medical Journal*, Nov. 9, October.

Westergaard, John. (1978) Social Policy and Class Inequality: Some Notes on Welfare State Limits, in Ralph Miliband and John Saville eds. *The Socialist Register*. New York: The Monthly Review Press.

Wilson, Elizabeth. (1980) Marxism and the Welfare State, *New Left Review*, No. 122, July.

Wolfe, A. (1977) *The Limits of Legitimacy*, Free Press.

Yaffe, David. (1973a) The Marxian Theory of Crisis, *Capital and The State. Economy and Society*, 22.

Yaffe, David. (1973b) The Crisis of Profitability: A Critique of the Glyne Sutcliffe Thesis, *New Left Review*, 80.